# Going to Mass
## *Becoming the Eucharist We Celebrate*

Jim McManus C.Ss.R.

Published by **Redemptorist Publications**
Alphonsus House, Chawton, Hampshire, GU34 3HQ, UK
Telephone +44 (0)1420 88222, Fax +44 (0)1420 88805
Email: rp@rpbooks.co.uk  Web: www.rpbooks.co.uk

A registered charity limited by guarantee
Registered in England 3261721

Copyright © Redemptorist Publications 2015
First published January 2015

Text by Jim McManus C.Ss.R.
Edited by Peter Edwards
Cover designed by Louise Hilton
Designed by Rosemarie Pink

ISBN 978-0-85231-428-9

A CIP catalogue record for this book is available from the British Library.

The publisher gratefully acknowledges permission to use the following copyright material:

Excerpts from the English translation and chants of *The Roman Missal* © 2010, International Commission on English in the Liturgy Corporation. All rights reserved.

Excerpts from THE JERUSALEM BIBLE, copyright © 1966 by Darton, Longman & Todd, Ltd and Doubleday, a division of Random House, Inc. Reprinted by permission.

Excerpts from *Vatican Council II: The Basic Sixteen Documents* (Northport, NY: Costello, 1996) © 1996 by Reverend Austin Flannery OP.

Printed by Stanley L Hunt (Printers) Limited, Northamptonshire, NN10 9UA

**Other titles by Jim McManus C.Ss.R.
available from Redemptorist Publications**

The Healing Power of the Sacraments

Healing in the Spirit

Hallowed Be Thy Name

All Generations Will Call Me Blessed

The Inside Job: A Spirituality of True Self-Esteem

I Am My Body: Blessed John Paul's Theology of the Body

Finding Forgiveness: Personal and Spiritual Perspectives
*(with Dr Stephanie Thornton)*

Searching for Serenity: Spirituality in Later Life
*(with Dr Stephanie Thornton)*

# Contents

# Preface

At the end of a retreat given for the priests of a diocese the bishop was thanking me. He said, "You began the retreat by quoting St Peter, saying that you saw your task as one of reminding us of what we already knew. But I think most of us are saying that what you said about the Eucharist was new to us." The words that I quoted from St Peter were, "I will always go on recalling the same truths to you, even though you already know them and are firmly fixed in these truths. I am sure it is my duty… to keep stirring you up with reminders" (2 Peter 1:12-13). We need someone to "stir us up with reminders" because aspects of the wonderful truth that we believe can slip out of our awareness and become lost amid the preoccupations of life.

We never take our knowledge of the Mass for granted or assume that because we were brought up in the Catholic faith or received instruction in it later in life we know all we need to know about our greatest act of worship. I was surprised and greatly encouraged when a very learned priest said to me at the end of a retreat, "You should really write a full book on that conference you gave us on the Eucharist. Much of it was quite new to me." The truth about the Mass is never stale.[1] It always has the quality of newness about it. *The Catechism of the Catholic Church* says, "The Eucharist is the sum and the summary of our faith."[2] When we are exploring the Mass we are entering into the depth of the mystery of our faith.

As we explore the Mass together in this book I pray that the words of the poet T.S. Eliot will ring true in your ears:

> We shall not cease from exploration.
> And the end of all our exploring
> Will be to arrive where we started
> And know the place for the first time.[3]

---

1  I will use the words Mass and Eucharist interchangeably in this book.

2  *Catechism of the Catholic Church*, 1327.

3  T.S. Eliot, "Little Gidding", in *Four Quartets* (London: Faber & Faber, 2001).

In this book we will explore what we are actually doing when we say, "We are going to Mass." The first activity we engage in is, of course, gathering together, the assembling as God's people to worship God. We devote the first chapter to reflecting on the meaning of this gathering.

As we worship God during the celebration of Mass we engage in four specific activities: we listen, we respond, we offer and we receive. In the second chapter we will reflect on what we are doing as we listen to God's word and as we respond to the God who speaks to us. The third chapter will explore the significance of offering our gifts of bread and wine to God and placing them on the altar in preparation for the great Eucharistic Prayer in which they will become for us the Body and Blood of Christ. That is the mystery of our faith. In the fourth chapter we will reflect on the meaning of the words we use as we proclaim this mystery of faith: "We proclaim your Death, O Lord, and profess your Resurrection until you come again." We devote the fifth chapter to reflecting on what we are doing as we receive Holy Communion.

The prayers of the Mass express the faith of the Church in this great mystery. We will devote the sixth chapter to examining in some detail the meaning of these prayers. We will be asking ourselves: Do we really conform our minds to the truth expressed in these prayers? Many of the prayers of the Mass are for health of mind and body. The seventh chapter explores the healing power of the Eucharist in our lives. In the final chapter we will explore the meaning of the words with which the congregation is sent forth at the end of Mass, "Go and announce the Gospel of the Lord." We will reflect on the Mass and the New Evangelisation.

My aim throughout this book is to help you to get in touch with your own feelings and to "stir you up with reminders" about this great mystery of our faith as you go to Mass and as you celebrate the holy Eucharist with your parish community.

Over the past fifty years as a priest I have had the wonderful grace of preaching on the Eucharist in Africa and Asia, in Australia and New Zealand, in the United States of America and Canada and, of course, throughout Britain and Ireland. On all continents I have encountered the same faith in the Mass, the same enthusiasm for entering more deeply into the mystery of the Mass and the same gratitude from people for preaching to them about the Mass. They will never know how their kind words of appreciation encouraged me to write this book. But the fact that they found what I said about the Mass helpful for their own understanding and devotion gave me the motivation to write this book on the Mass in the year when I celebrate my Golden Jubilee in the priesthood. It is my way of saying thanks to all the wonderful people who have ministered to me by their encouraging words during these past fifty years.

I am grateful to Fr Charles Corrigan, my Rector here at St Mary's, who read the manuscript and made many helpful suggestions. Also, I wish to thank all the members of my community at St Mary's for their unfailing, fraternal and prayerful support.

Fr Jim McManus C.Ss.R.
St Mary's
Clapham Common
London SW4 7AP

# Chapter One

# Going to Mass:
# entering the sacred assembly

What do Catholics do? The simplest and the clearest answer to that question is to say that *Catholics go to Mass*. That answer contains, in shorthand, all that Catholics believe, how they seek to live and all that they are invited by God to do. Our whole faith, the whole content of our faith, is involved in the Mass. And, indeed, our whole understanding of who we are as persons, as a community, as a Church, is expressed in that one action of *going to Mass*. These may be surprising statements. But, as we look at what the Mass means for Catholics, and what celebrating the Mass requires of us, we will be able to see more clearly that they are correct. Going to Mass is the action that expresses our faith in what Jesus did at the Last Supper when he took the bread and said, "This is my body which will be given for you; do this as a memorial of me," and when he took the cup and said, "This cup is the new covenant in my blood which will be poured out for you" (Luke 22:19-20). We are asked by Christ to do with our lives what he did with his. We are asked to become the Eucharist we celebrate. As the *Catechism of the Catholic Church* says, "The Eucharist is the sum and the summary of our faith: 'Our way of thinking is attuned to the Eucharist, and the Eucharist... confirms our way of thinking.'"[1] Our way of living, of acting, of relating to others is also attuned to the Eucharist. Through celebrating the Eucharist our life becomes Eucharistic.

The Orthodox theologian Alexander Schmemann expressed this well when he wrote:

> When I say I am going to church, it means I am going into the assembly of the faithful in order, together with them,

---

1  *Catechism of the Catholic Church*, 1327.

to *constitute the Church*, in order to be what I became on the day of my baptism – a *member*, in the fullest, absolute meaning of the term, of the body of Christ.[2]

Going to Mass means, in the first place, joining the assembly of the faithful, the sacred assembly, that gathers in Christ's name to worship God our Creator and Father, by engaging in four activities, namely, listening to God's word, responding with praise and thanks, offering our gifts and ourselves to God and receiving Christ our Saviour in Holy Communion. These four activities contain our full participation in the celebration of the Mass.

When I was a boy people used to talk about wearing "their Sunday best". These were their best clothes, which they put on when they went to church. But our true "Sunday best" is not our outward garments but the inner faith and grace that enable us to enter into the assembly of the faithful where we become "one body, one spirit in Christ"[3]. The Sunday congregation, gathered in Christ's name, be it large or small, is the Church of Christ. Christ is no less present in the assembly of thirty than he was present in the assembly of the three million when Pope Francis celebrated Mass in Rio for World Youth Day in July 2013. That coming together, great or small, is the first act of our liturgical celebration of the Mass. As Schmemann writes:

> "The *assembly as Church*" is in reality the first liturgical act, the foundation of the entire liturgy; and unless one understands this, one cannot understand the rest of the celebration.[4]

The Second Vatican Council restored this true sense of the liturgy to the Church in our time:

> Liturgical services have to do with the whole body, the church. They make it visible and have effects on it.[5]

---

2  Alexander Schmemann, *The Eucharist: Sacrament of the Kingdom* (New York: St Vladimir's Seminary Press, 2000), p. 23.
3  Eucharistic Prayer III.
4  Schmemann, *The Eucharist*, p. 23.
5  *Sacrosanctum Concilium*, Constitution on the Sacred Liturgy, 26.

We assemble, not as a group of individuals but as Church, as the body of Christ, to *celebrate* the Mass, and not just to *be present at* the Mass. Our *going* to Mass becomes *celebrating* the Mass, which is the action of the whole assembly. As the General Instruction of the Roman Missal says:

> In the celebration of Mass the faithful form a holy people, a people of God's own possession and a royal priesthood, so that they may give thanks to God and offer the unblemished sacrificial Victim not only by means of the hands of the Priest but also together with him and so that they may learn to offer their very selves.[6]

Notice those two fundamental offerings that we all make at Mass:

- we offer "the unblemished sacrificial victim" with the priest;
- and we offer ourselves to God.

We assemble for Mass to make this twofold offering, not as isolated individuals, but as members of the one body of Christ, the community of the faithful, the Sunday congregation. As the General Instruction of the Roman Missal emphasises:

> [The faithful] are to form one body, whether in hearing the Word of God, or in taking part in the prayers and in the singing, or above all by the common offering of the Sacrifice and by participating together at the Lord's table.[7]

It is not just the priest who is offering "the bread and wine". The whole congregation are offering the bread and wine with the priest. And, most importantly of all, we all offer ourselves to God as we offer our gifts of bread and wine. The priest cannot make that offering of ourselves for us; we have to do it for ourselves. St Paul said, "Think of God's mercy... and worship him, I beg you, in a way that is worthy of thinking beings,

---

6  The General Instruction of the Roman Missal, 95.

7  Ibid., 96.

by offering your living bodies as a holy sacrifice, truly pleasing to God" (Romans 12:1). On St Paul's exhortation to make this offering of our bodies, Benedict XVI commented:

> In these words the new worship appears as a total self-offering made in communion with the whole Church. The Apostle's insistence on the offering of our bodies emphasizes the concrete human reality of a worship which is anything but disincarnate.[8]

**The first liturgical act of the Mass is assembling as Church**

Our great act of worship of God has already begun as we begin to assemble. God's people are gathering before our eyes. Some we may know, others may be strangers, but we have the one thing in common: we are all members of Christ and Christ is in each of us. So, as the congregation begins to assemble, the great act of worship has begun. In fact, as you begin to get ready to leave your house and make your way to the church, your celebration has already begun. You are making your way to join God's holy people where you become one body with all those gathering. If you were asked to prove your identity on your way into the gathering of the faithful you would produce your baptismal certificate. Baptism opens the door to the full sacramental life of the Church. We are reborn as children of God in the sacrament of baptism. As the Catechism teaches:

> By virtue of our Baptism, the first sacrament of the faith, the Holy Spirit in the Church communicates to us, intimately and personally, the life that originates in the Father and is offered to us in the Son.[9]

Going to Mass means that we are publicly declaring that as baptised members of the Church we have a right and a duty to join the assembly of the faithful in worshipping God. We are affirming our true identity as sons or daughters of God.

---

8  Benedict XVI, *Heart of the Christian Life* (San Francisco: Ignatius Press, 2010), p. 75.
9  *Catechism of the Catholic Church*, 683.

## Manifestation of the Church

It is as God's holy people, as the holy assembly, that we gather for the Mass. We have become the visible Church. As the Second Vatican Council said, the Church is "a people made one by the unity of the Father, the Son and the Holy Spirit".[10] Our gathering together to celebrate the Mass manifests this unity of the Church. Indeed, it is through our celebration of the Mass that we express in our lives the whole mystery of Christ. The Second Vatican Council reminded us:

> The liturgy, through which "the work of our redemption takes place", especially in the divine sacrifice of the Eucharist, is supremely effective in enabling the faithful to express in their lives and portray to others the mystery of Christ and the real nature of the true church.[11]

We are not just worshipping God by going to Mass, we are also manifesting to ourselves and to others the "real nature of the true church". As Schmemann wrote:

> The Eucharist is not "one of the sacraments" or one of the services, but the very manifestation and fulfilment of the Church in all her power, sanctity and fullness.[12]

The *Catechism of the Catholic Church* agrees with what Schmemann wrote. It reminds us that:

> The Eucharist is "the source and summit of the Christian life". The other sacraments, and indeed all ecclesiastical ministries and works of the apostolate, are bound up with the Eucharist and are oriented toward it. For in the blessed Eucharist is contained the whole spiritual good of the Church, namely Christ himself, our Pasch.[13]

As we gather for the Mass this manifestation of the Church begins to happen. Christ is as truly present within a small congregation of a few dozen as he is present within a congregation of thousands.

---

10 *Lumen Gentium*, Dogmatic Constitution on the Church, 4.

11 *Sacrosanctum Concilium*, 2.

12 Schmemann, *The Eucharist*, p. 25.

13 *Catechism of the Catholic Church*, 1324.

Both congregations, the small and the large, are manifestations of the Church and embody the presence of Christ. The Mass that is celebrated by the small community of ten gives the same glory to God as the Mass celebrated by a community of ten thousand.

### As if we had been present there

Writing about why Jesus chose to leave us the Eucharist, St John Paul II said:

> When the Church celebrates the Eucharist, the memorial of her Lord's death and resurrection, this central event of salvation becomes really present and "the work of our redemption is carried out". This sacrifice is so decisive for the salvation of the human race that Jesus Christ offered it and returned to the Father *only after he had left us a means of sharing in it* as if we had been present there.[14]

What a wonderful insight John Paul gives us when he says Jesus didn't return to the Father until he had left us the opportunity of sharing in his great sacrifice for our salvation "as if we had been present there"! That is what "going to Mass" means; it is going to be present at the hour of our redemption. We are at no disadvantage because we were not present at the table in the Upper Room in Jerusalem on that first Holy Thursday evening when Jesus gave us the gift of his Body and Blood in the Eucharist. Each time we gather to celebrate the Mass we are present at the same sacrifice of his Body and Blood under the appearance of the bread and wine. At each Mass Jesus says to us, "Take this, all of you, and eat of it, for this is my Body," and, "Take this, all of you, and drink from it, for this is the chalice of my Blood of the new and eternal covenant." We share in Christ's hour of sacrifice. As Benedict XVI says:

> Jesus left us the task of entering into his "hour". The Eucharist draws us into Jesus' act of self-oblation... we

---

14 John Paul II, *Ecclesia de Eucharistia*, 11.

enter into the very dynamic of his self-giving. Jesus "draws us into himself".[15]

Christ's hour, the hour of our salvation, becomes present to us. As scripture says, Jesus "offered himself as the perfect sacrifice to God through the eternal Spirit" (Hebrews 9:14) and that offering remains in the presence of the Father for ever. As we celebrate the Mass, the redeeming sacrifice of Christ becomes present on the altar. We enter into Christ's hour, into his great redeeming love, as he offers himself to the Father for our salvation. Since Jesus' death and resurrection are the central realities of our faith, we had to have some way of drawing close to them, remembering them, receiving through them the gift of our redemption and sanctification. That is why Jesus gave us himself as the "bread of life" in the Eucharist.

The Mass is the "mystery of our faith". The truth that the risen Lord Jesus Christ makes his death and resurrection present to us under the form of bread and wine can only be received through a living faith. We would not expect a person who had no faith to believe this truth, because this truth cannot be known by reason or logic. It can only be known through faith, through the inner enlightenment of the Holy Spirit.

Christ is already present in the gathering congregation. It is he who is inviting us to come to his table. Without his invitation we would not be making our way into the worshipping assembly of the faithful. This coming together on a Sunday as the sacred assembly of the worshipping community can be a noisy and a distracting time. If we are not attentive to what we are doing we can gather, just as we gather for other events, waiting for the action to happen. But in our Sunday assembly the action is already happening. Jesus said, "I tell you solemnly once again, if two of you on earth agree to ask anything at all, it will be granted to you by my Father in heaven. For where two or three meet in my name, I shall be there with them"

---

15 Benedict XVI, *Sacramentum Caritatis*, 11.

(Matthew 18:19-20). We don't have to wait, as it were, for Jesus to become present on the altar at the consecration of the bread and wine. Jesus is already present in our midst as we gather. Jesus is the host of the Eucharistic banquet and he is there to welcome each one of us when we enter into "the sacred assembly", our Sunday congregation. As he welcomes us, we should respond in prayer and thanksgiving and silent adoration. A notice in an Anglican church expresses this well: "Talk to God before Mass and to your neighbour after Mass."

### We are Church[16]

Entering into the building that we call the church requires no faith at all. We walk in and out of many buildings every week. But entering into the "sacred assembly", the congregation gathered for the celebration of the Mass, does require faith. As we enter the "sacred assembly" the first person there to meet us is Jesus. When we start to assemble, we are not just waiting for the priest to come out and begin Mass. We are already gathered as the Church, with Christ in our midst. We are the Church because Jesus Christ is in our midst, uniting us as one body, his body. If we miss this presence of Christ in our midst it will be difficult to enter into the mystery of the Mass. If we do not consciously remind ourselves that we are not just *in* the church, in the building, but that *we are* the Church, we are the "sacred assembly" of God's people, we are gathered as the body of Christ, we will probably find Mass boring. We have to engage our faith on this deep level of believing that as we gather for the Mass we are gathering, not just as individuals, but as the body of Christ. St Paul said, "Now you together are Christ's body; but each of you is a different part of it" (1 Corinthians 12:27).

### The "sacrament" of the congregation

The assembling of the faithful for the Sunday celebration of Mass is a sacramental reality because it is in and through this gathering that Christ becomes present to us. We can, therefore, speak of the "sacrament of the congregation" or the "sacrament of the sacred

---

16 In the New Testament the word "church" always means the people in a city who believed in Christ. St Paul addressed his letter to "the church of God in Corinth" (1 Corinthians 1:1). Gradually the word "church" began to mean the building where "the church of God" met to celebrate the Eucharist.

assembly". Very often this is the sacrament we fail to see. We define a sacrament as "the outward sign of inward grace". When we look around at the congregation gathering for Mass we are seeing the outward sign, the men and women and children, coming to the Mass. We can, however, fail to see in faith the inward grace that this gathering of brothers and sisters embodies, namely, God's transforming grace that makes those gathering the very body of Christ. If we miss this sacramental dimension of the congregation we will struggle with the rest of the Mass. While we may be devoutly saying our own prayers, we will not be praying as "one body, one Spirit in Christ".

Going to Mass is always a decision and act made as part of a community.[17] As individuals we decide to assume our communal identity, our Christian identity, and become part of the sacred assembly where we are welcomed by the priest as "brothers and sisters" and where all the prayers are communal. Listen to the way we pray: "We praise you, we bless you, we glorify you, we give you thanks for your great glory." As we join the "sacred assembly" we consciously begin to think in terms of "us" and not in terms of "me". Perhaps we could more consciously cultivate this sense of community, this sense of being one with the whole congregation. All the prayers of the Mass are said in this communal spirit and voice. The only time we use the singular form is when we say, "I confess to almighty God and to you, my brothers and sisters, that I have greatly sinned..." or when we profess our faith in the Creed with the words "I believe..." or just before Holy Communion when we say, "Lord, I am not worthy..."

**Why do we gather to celebrate Mass?**
We come together as a community to celebrate Mass for the glory of God. That is our first duty towards God, to worship and adore our Father and Creator. We pray in the Preface of Eucharistic Prayer II: "It is truly right and just, our duty and our salvation, always and everywhere to give you thanks, Father most holy, through your

---

17 Even if the priest is on his own, without any members of the congregation, the Church encourages him to celebrate Mass. Benedict XVI said, "To this end I join the Synod Fathers in recommending 'the daily celebration of Mass, even when the faithful are not present'. This recommendation is consistent with the objectively infinite value of the Eucharist, and is motivated by the Mass's unique spiritual fruitfulness" (*Sacramentum Caritatis*, 80).

beloved Son, Jesus Christ…" What is happening when we give God glory? What is the glory that we offer to God? St Irenaeus, who was martyred around AD 202, gave us this definition of the glory of God: "the glory of God is the person fully alive".[18] In gathering to give God glory, something happens in us. We become more fully alive in the Spirit. Whatever is opposed to being fully alive within us is being dealt with. If it is a sin, it is being forgiven; if it is a wound of sin, we are being healed; if it is some form of bondage in our lives, we are being delivered from it. If God is being glorified, we are being changed.

The transforming grace of the Mass is offered to us as we consciously participate in the celebration of the whole Mass. This full and conscious participation in the Mass is crucial for our spiritual lives as individuals and as a community. The Second Vatican Council put it this way:

> It is very much the wish of the church that all the faithful should be led to take that full, conscious, and active part in liturgical celebrations which is demanded by the very nature of the liturgy, and to which the Christian people, "a chosen race, a royal priesthood, a holy nation, a redeemed people" (1 Peter 2:9. 4-5) have a right and to which they are bound by reason of their Baptism.[19]

Four different activities constitute our full participation in the Mass: *we listen*, *we respond*, *we offer* and *we receive*. Each of these activities constitutes an essential part of our participation in the Mass. We know that we don't go to Mass in a purely spectator role. Nor do we go to Mass just to say our own private prayers. We have to participate; we have to get involved in the action of the Mass; we have to cultivate the sense of community and of being in communion. The liturgy itself is called in our Catholic tradition "the sacred action". Jesus said, "Do this in memory of me." Our Eucharistic celebration is doing just that, doing what Jesus did. As the Second Vatican Council said:

18 St Irenaeus, *Against Heresies*, IV, 20, 5-7.
19 *Sacrosanctum Concilium*, 14

The church, therefore, spares no effort in trying to ensure that, when present at this mystery of faith, Christian believers should not be there as strangers or silent spectators. On the contrary, having a good grasp of it through the rites and prayers, they should take part in the sacred action, actively, fully aware, and devoutly. They should be formed by God's word, and be nourished at the table of the Lord's Body. They should give thanks to God. Offering the immaculate victim, not only through the hands of the priest but also together with him, they should learn to offer themselves. Through Christ, the Mediator, they should be drawn day by day into ever more perfect union with God and each other, so that finally God may be all in all.[20]

Notice how the Vatican Council describes our participation in the Mass. We are not "silent spectators", we take part "in the sacred action", we offer the Mass "together with the priest" and, our deepest participation in the mystery, "we offer ourselves". As we gather for the celebration of the Mass we take part in the "sacred action".

**The examination of conscience: social implications**

At the very beginning of Mass the priest invites us to enter into our hearts, to become aware of how we have been living our life of relationship with God, with Jesus and with one another. Benedict XVI reminded us:

Being a Christian is not the result of an ethical choice or a lofty idea, but the encounter with an event, a person, which gives life a new horizon and a decisive direction.[21]

We are assembling for Mass not just because "we are Catholics" but because we have "encountered", we have met, we have got to know the Lord Jesus Christ. We are gathering in the church

---

20 *Sacrosanctum Concilium*, 48.
21 Benedict XVI, *Deus Caritas Est*, 1

because Christ has invited us to come to his table. The first thing we are asked to do is to look at our relationship with Jesus and to consider well what he says to us. Jesus says to us, "I shall not call you servants any more... I call you friends" (John 15:15). It is as the friends of Jesus, therefore, that we are now invited to examine our conscience. This is a very personal act. The community cannot do that for us. Each of us has to do that examination for himself or herself. But, although each of us has to do it for himself or herself, we cannot and should not attempt to do it by ourselves. We do it in the awareness of our friendship with Jesus. As we look at our own sinfulness and miseries, we always keep our eyes fixed on his mercy and love, which wash away all our sins as we repent. We do not doubt his mercy or his power to cleanse us from all our sins. Because we are his friends, Jesus says to us, "Love one another, as I have loved you" (John 15:12). We know from the experience of our own selfishness that we are greatly challenged by this invitation from Jesus. Can I really love others in the way that Jesus loves me? Again, we acknowledge that, although each of us is invited by Jesus to love in this extraordinary way, we cannot do it by ourselves, We can love in this way only through the power of the Holy Spirit. That is the power that Jesus promised to each of us when he said, "You will receive power when the Holy Spirit comes on you, and then you will be my witnesses" (Acts 1:8). Benedict XVI gave us this description of what happens when we become witnesses:

> We become witnesses when, through our actions, words and way of being, Another makes himself present.[22]

When we truly love one another, Christ becomes present to us and to those whom we love. If you can imagine a person who loves nobody, but seeks only his or her own advantage in each situation, that person cannot be a witness to Christ. Only self-giving love, the gift of the Holy Spirit, empowers the person to become the witness.

---

22 Benedict XVI, *Sacramentum Caritatis*, 85.

We are invited to honestly examine the quality of our love for all our brothers and sisters.

Loving as Jesus loves expresses itself in the way we help those in need: those who are poor, homeless, hungry. Indeed, if we refuse to help them, Jesus says we are refusing to help him: "I was hungry and you never gave me food; I was thirsty and you never gave me anything to drink" and "in so far as you neglected to do this to one of the least of these, you neglected to do it to me" (Matthew 25:42-45). Our examination of conscience is not simply a private affair. It has enormous social consequences. We are being asked, indeed challenged, to look afresh at the society we are living in. Who cares for those who are hungry and without a roof over their heads? Do we feel any responsibility towards those who are poor and those who are outcasts? If we do, how are we showing it? How are we standing up for their rights? Am I and is my community on the side of those who are poor and outcast? The Mass is not an escape from our responsibilities towards one another! It is the very opposite. This was St John Paul II's desire for the Year of the Eucharist which the Church celebrated during 2004–2005:

> Can we not make this *Year of the Eucharist* an occasion for diocesan and parish communities to commit themselves in a particular way to responding with fraternal solicitude to one of the many forms of poverty present in our world? I think for example of the tragedy of hunger which plagues hundreds of millions of human beings, the diseases which afflict developing countries, the loneliness of the elderly, the hardships faced by the unemployed, the struggles of immigrants. These are evils which are present – albeit to a different degree – even in areas of immense wealth. We cannot delude ourselves: by our mutual love and, in particular, by our concern for those in need we will be recognized as true followers of Christ (cf. John 13:35;

Matthew 25:31-46). This will be the criterion by which the authenticity of our Eucharistic celebrations is judged.[23]

The very "authenticity of our Eucharistic celebrations" depends not on beautiful liturgy, uplifting music and singing, but on the Eucharistic community's concern for those who are poor and marginalised in our society. We see this true love manifest in our Catholic communities whenever tragedies like earthquakes or tsunami strike. Catholic congregations respond with great generosity. Our Catholic communities, comprising all shades of political opinions, would agree with Pope Francis when he writes, "The Church 'cannot and must not remain on the sidelines in the fight for justice'." [24]

### The whole human family is involved in the Mass

As we prepare ourselves to celebrate Mass we are called to honestly face how we are behaving towards everyone, especially towards those most in need. The priest says, "Brothers and sisters, let us acknowledge our sins, and so prepare ourselves to celebrate the sacred mysteries." In the "sacred assembly" before God we seek to be honest, to acknowledge in our hearts our sinful and selfish failures, and to ask God's pardon as we pray for the grace to improve. Our biggest failure seems to be our blindness to the great truth encoded in that greeting of "brothers and sisters". The priest acknowledges us as brothers and sisters in the presence of God, but do we believe this and do we live as brothers and sisters in the Lord? This relationship with each other is not confined to those in the congregation. It embraces all humankind because Jesus became a brother to every human being. The Second Vatican Council said, "By his incarnation, he, the Son of God, has in a certain way united himself with each individual."[25] As the members of Christ's body in this world we are united with each individual, just as Jesus is. Just as there is no one outside the love and the mercy of God, so there is no one outside our love and mercy. Indeed, the Second Vatican Council reminded us that,

---

23 John Paul II, *Mane Nobiscum Domine*, 28

24 Pope Francis, *Evangelii Gaudium*, 183.

25 *Gaudium et Spes*, Pastoral Constitution on the Church in the Modern World, 22.

> Since Christ died for everyone, and since all are in fact
> called to one and the same destiny, which is divine, we
> must hold that the Holy Spirit offers to all the possibility
> of being made partners, in a way known to God, in the
> paschal mystery.[26]

God knows each human being and to each one God offers the gift of
salvation. As we gather to celebrate the great mystery of our salvation
we reflect on the love and mercy of God and on how we are showing
this love and mercy to all our brothers and sisters.

When we enter the sacred assembly to celebrate the Eucharist we
do so as brothers and sisters to every single human being. We seek
to see ourselves as Jesus sees himself. Jesus is the brother to every
human being who will ever be born into this world. In our celebration
of the Eucharist, the sacrifice of Christ for the whole world, our
horizon expands to embrace the whole human race. If we exclude
any person, or group, or nation from that embrace we are not yet
ready to celebrate the mystery of Christ giving his life for the whole
of humanity. We must first repent, acknowledge this as our sin, and
ask for God's mercy and forgiveness. We stand before God not just
with our friends, whom we find it very easy to love, but also with our
enemies, whom we find it hard to love. St John Paul II encourages
us in our weakness with these words:

> By sharing in the sacrifice of the Cross, the Christian
> partakes of Christ's self-giving love and is equipped and
> committed to live this same charity in all his thoughts and
> deeds.[27]

Going to Mass means opening our whole life to the transforming,
redeeming love of Christ, which enables us, despite all our sinful
weakness, to love as Christ loves. It is with that commitment that
we take our place at the table of the word of God.

---

26 *Gaudium et Spes*, 22.
27 John Paul II, *Veritatis Splendor*, 107.

# Chapter Two

# At the table of the word of God

We have to take our place at "two tables" while we are at Mass: the table of the word of God and the table of the Body of the Lord. We must be nourished at both tables. In fact, if we are not nourished at the table of the word of God it will be very difficult for us to find our true nourishment at the table of the Body of the Lord.

## The Liturgy of the Word

Listening to the word of God that is proclaimed in the first part of the Mass is called "the Liturgy of the Word". It is not an optional exercise. If we really desire to enter deeply into the mystery of the Mass and derive full spiritual nourishment from the Mass, we have to give our full and undivided attention to Christ who speaks to us. We listen in faith to what God is saying because without hearing his word we will not be able to enter into the mystery of the Mass. As Benedict XVI said:

> Word and Eucharist are so deeply bound together that we cannot understand one without the other.[1]

Listening in faith requires cultivating the conscious awareness that it is Christ himself who is speaking to us as the scripture is being proclaimed. We have to give him our full and undivided attention. We are so easily distracted. St Luke describes how a very good friend of Jesus was distracted as he was teaching:

> In the course of their journey he came to a village, and a woman named Martha welcomed him into her house. She had a sister called Mary, who sat down at the Lord's feet and listened to him speaking. Now Martha who was distracted with all the serving said, "Lord, do you not

---

1 Benedict XVI, *Verbum Domini*, 55.

care that my sister is leaving me to do the serving all by myself? Please tell her to help me." But the Lord answered: "Martha, Martha," he said "you worry and fret about so many things, and yet few are needed, indeed only one. It is Mary who has chosen the better part; it is not to be taken from her" (Luke 10:38-42).

The "better part" was that Mary had chosen to listen to the Lord as a disciple. The disciple sits at the Master's feet. But, as Eugene LaVerdiere points out:

Being at the Lord's feet doesn't mean that Mary was not working. It does mean that she was not distracted by the ministry or worried and fretting about many things. Her attention was fixed on the word of the Lord, the one thing necessary, which gives meaning to every other aspect of ministry.[2]

Jesus, however, speaks very affectionately to his friend and hostess by addressing her by name and repeating her name: "Martha, Martha". The repetition of her name meant that Jesus really wanted her to pay attention because what he had to say was very important for her. He wanted her to be his disciple too, not just his friend and generous hostess. He had the words of eternal life. The same Lord is teaching as the scriptures are being read during the Mass. Without a conscious effort at listening with our heart we will find ourselves "distracted", "worrying and fretting about so many things" while the word of God is being proclaimed. At those times you may well hear the Lord calling you by name and repeating your name as if to say, "Please listen to me."

### Root of sin

As we saw in the last chapter, we begin the Mass by asking God's forgiveness for our sins. The root cause of all our sins, Benedict XVI said, is our "refusal to hear the word of the Lord". He wrote:

---

2  Eugene LaVerdiere, *Dining in the Kingdom of God: The Origins of the Eucharist in the Gospel of Luke* (Chicago: Liturgy Training Publications, 1994), p. 85.

> We are... offered the merciful possibility of redemption and the start of a new life in Christ. For this reason it is important that the faithful be taught to acknowledge that the root of sin lies in the refusal to hear the word of the Lord and accept in Jesus, the Word of God, the forgiveness which opens us to salvation.[3]

If the root of sin is the refusal to hear the word of God, the eagerness to hear God's word is the great sign of grace, of our willingness to live in God's grace, to live by God's word. It is with that eagerness that we seek to listen to the word during Mass. We know from our own experience that it can be quite difficult to pay attention to the readings from the holy scriptures during Mass. Sometimes, too, it is very hard to hear what the reader is saying. Also, as we know, some of the readings, especially from the Old Testament, can be quite difficult to follow. We may be unfamiliar with the background of the Old Testament readings.

**The Second Vatican Council on the word of God**

While it is very helpful to have some knowledge of the Bible we do not need to be experts on the Bible as we listen to the word of God. We have to remind ourselves that God is coming to speak to us, and ask for the grace to welcome God's word. As the Second Vatican Council says:

> In the sacred books the Father who is in heaven comes lovingly to meet his children, and talks with them. And such is the force and power of the word of God that it is the church's support and strength, imparting robustness to the faith of its daughters and sons and providing food for their souls. It is a pure and unfailing fount of spiritual life.[4]

The first thing we have to realise each time we hear the scriptures proclaimed at Mass is that these words are not just the words of

---

3  Benedict XVI, *Verbum Domini*, 26.
4  *Dei Verbum*, Dogmatic Constitution on Divine Revelation, 21.

some ancient writer, a Jeremiah or a St Paul or a St Peter, but that the Lord himself, using the words of those ancient writers, is now speaking to us. St Paul, for instance, in writing to the Church in Rome or in Corinth, was teaching them the faith in Christ that they had accepted. But the deeper reality in what St Paul had to say was the fact that the Holy Spirit used his words to speak, not just to the first-century Christians, to whom he was writing, but to the twenty-first-century Christians who hear his words today. Through St Paul's words the Holy Spirit speaks to us each time we hear them proclaimed at Mass or each time we read St Paul's letters privately. And, of course, when the Gospel is being proclaimed it is Jesus himself who is speaking directly to us.

Our interior attitude as we listen to the scripture being proclaimed should always be, "Speak, Lord, your servant is listening." I hear the words with my ears, I receive them into my mind, but it is the Holy Spirit who speaks the divine truth expressed by the human words in my heart. If my heart is closed to the word, I may hear it with my ears, but it will not penetrate to the depths of my being. That is why Benedict XVI could say that the root of sin is the refusal to hear the word of God.

When the reader at Mass concludes the reading, he or she says, "The word of the Lord", and we all respond, "Thanks be to God." In that moment we are professing our faith in God's word, acknowledging to one another in "the sacred assembly" that we believe that scripture is God's word and that God speaks to us in the word of scripture. Christ speaks to us directly through the word. As the Second Vatican Council said:

> [Christ] is present in his word since it is he himself who speaks when the holy scriptures are read in church.[5]

But how do we listen to Christ speaking to us?

---

5  *Sacrosanctum Concilium*, Constitution on the Sacred Liturgy, 7.

Catholics have wonderful faith in the sacramental presence of Jesus in the consecrated bread and wine. We treat the Blessed Sacrament with profound respect. But, I believe, we struggle with Christ's presence in the word and therefore we may not listen to the word with the same devotion with which we attend to the consecration. The real renewal of our liturgy will happen for each of us when we discover who it is who is speaking to us as the scriptures are being read in the Mass. This truth was brought home to me years ago as I was trying to respond to the oft-repeated comment that the Mass is boring. I was trying to think how we could "jazz up" the Mass, to make it more exciting, when it dawned on me that the Mass will be boring to those who do not hear the word of God. The whole first part of the Mass, twenty minutes or more, is devoted, in one way or another, to the proclamation of the word. If we sit through the readings, waiting patiently for the Liturgy of the Eucharist to begin, we will certainly become very bored. This is where the image that the Second Vatican Council introduced is so helpful: we don't just sit listening to a word, we sit at "the table of the word of God", being fed and nourished by the word. Our celebration of the Mass will be impoverished if we do not develop all our capacity for listening in faith and welcoming God's word into our heart.

**The Emmaus experience**
The story of the two disciples on the road to Emmaus on the first Easter morning teaches us the importance of listening to the word of God. St Luke tells us that these two disciples were walking away from Jerusalem, sad and downhearted, and they were discussing what had happened to Jesus on Good Friday. They didn't recognise Jesus as he approached them and walked alongside them. When he asked them what they had been discussing as they walked along, they said,

> All about Jesus of Nazareth… who proved he was a great prophet by the things he said and did in the sight of God and the whole people… Our own hope had been that he would be the one to set Israel free (Luke 24:19-21).

Their hopes had been dashed. They were talking about Jesus in the past tense. Jesus had been crucified and buried. It was all over. Then Jesus began to teach them:

> Starting with Moses and going through all the prophets, he explained to them the passages throughout the scriptures that were about himself. When they drew near to the village to which they were going, he made as if to go on; but they pressed him to stay with them… So he went in to stay with them (Luke 24:27-29).

They offered Jesus hospitality and prepared a meal for him. St Luke tells us what happened:

> Now while he was with them at table, he took the bread and said the blessing; then he broke it and handed it to them. And their eyes were opened and they recognised him; but he had vanished from their sight. Then they said to one another, "Did not our hearts burn within us as he talked to us on the road and explained the scriptures to us?" (Luke 24:30-32).

That is the experience we all need. We need our hearts to be set on fire through hearing the word of God proclaimed in the Mass.

While good music and joyful singing are a great help in our celebration of the Mass, they are no substitute for hearing the word of God and being nourished by that word. Jesus, the Word of God made flesh, tells us that we do not "live on bread alone but on every word that comes from the mouth of God" (Matthew 4:4). The word of God is at the very centre of our life, of our very identity, because our deepest identity is that we are the sons and daughters of God our Father. As Benedict XVI said:

> We were created in the word and we live in the word; we cannot understand ourselves unless we are open to this dialogue.[6]

## The Holy Spirit and the word of God

At the table of the word of God during Mass we have a sacred moment to hear what God the Father is saying to us. This requires an effort on our part. First of all we have to give our full attention to the proclamation of the word. Our thoughts, of course, can be elsewhere as the reader begins. We have to challenge our lack of attention. God is coming to speak to us and we should cling to every word. We should cultivate the hunger for the word of God that the prophet Jeremiah had when he said, "When your words came, I devoured them: your word was my delight and the joy of my heart" (Jeremiah 15:16). Do we listen at the table of the word of God in a way that enables us to be nourished by what God is saying to us? If we don't listen in faith, in the awareness that God the Father is speaking to us, we will not be able to receive the word of God as "our delight and the joy of our heart". That is why it is so helpful to develop the habit of praying for the Holy Spirit to enlighten us as the reader makes his or her way to the ambo or the lectern to proclaim the word. We could pray in the words of the young Samuel, "Speak, Lord, your servant is listening" (1 Samuel 3:10) or we could simply say, "Holy Spirit, enlighten my mind and heart as I listen to the holy scriptures being proclaimed." God is speaking to us as the scriptures are being proclaimed but if we do not allow the Holy Spirit to open our ears we will not hear. There is a very close correspondence between the action of the Holy Spirit at the consecration of the bread and wine and the hearing of the word of God. As Alexander Schmemann wrote:

---

6  Benedict XVI, *Verbum Domini*, 22.

> Like the consecration of the gifts, *understanding and acceptance* of the word depend not on us, not only on our desires, but above all on the sacramental transformation of the "eyes of our mind", on the coming of the Holy Spirit.[7]

Without that light of the Holy Spirit we will not be able to hear what God is saying to us in the Mass.

We have to be patient with ourselves as we try to hear and understand the scriptures being proclaimed, especially readings from the Old Testament. Many of us have little knowledge of the historical and cultural background to the Old Testament. We believe, nevertheless, that our faith began with the one we call "our father in faith" – with Abraham, the father of the Jewish people, God's people. Jesus, in his response to the Sadducees, spoke of "the God of Abraham, the God of Isaac and the God of Jacob" (Luke 20:37). Jesus is the one in whom all the promises made to Abraham, Isaac and Jacob and their descendants, which we find in the Old Testament, are fulfilled. As St Paul said, "However many the promises God made, the Yes to them all is in him" (2 Corinthians 1:20). The Old Testament hands on to us all the promises God made to God's people in the history of their salvation. We are encouraged today to make every effort to become more familiar with it. That is why the Church now invites us to listen to readings from the Old Testament most Sundays. As the Second Vatican Council said:

> The treasures of the Bible are to be opened up more lavishly so that a richer fare may be provided for the faithful at the table of God's word.[8]

### Listening in faith

St Jerome said, "We cannot come to an understanding of Scripture without the assistance of the Holy Spirit who inspired it."[9] As we allow the Holy Spirit to open our hearts we will begin to hear the

---

7  Alexander Schmemann, *The Eucharist: Sacrament of the Kingdom* (New York: St Vladimir's Seminary Press, 2000), p. 76.

8  *Sacrosanctum Concilium*, 51.

9  As quoted in Benedict XVI, *Verbum Domini*, 16.

words of scripture in a new way. The letter to the Hebrews tells us that "The word of God is something alive and active" (4:12). It is not a word from the past, about some situation in the past. It is spoken to us in the present. But without faith we will not be able to hear it as a personal word. St Thomas Aquinas said:

> The letter even of the Gospel would kill were there not the inward grace of healing faith.[10]

Without faith in Christ's presence in the Blessed Sacrament we cannot receive Holy Communion. Likewise, without faith we will not be able to hear the word of God as the scriptures are being proclaimed. Invoking the Holy Spirit to enlighten our minds as we listen to the scriptures being proclaimed is the necessary preparation for hearing the word of God.

Sometimes we can make the mistake of trying to leave all our troubles behind us when we come to Mass. But, as we will see in the next chapter, our troubles are the very thing that we bring to offer to God during Mass. Jesus invites us in this way: "Come to me, all you who labour and are overburdened, and I will give you rest" (Matthew 11:28). We bring our burdens to leave them in God's presence. The word that God speaks to us during Mass is addressed to us in the midst of our joys and sorrows, our successes and our failures. We listen to the proclamation of the word of God from the depth of our experience because the life-giving word of God has the answer to all our problems. Benedict XVI reminded us:

> It is decisive, from the pastoral standpoint, to present the word of God in its capacity to enter into dialogue with the everyday problems which people face… we need to make every effort to share the word of God as an openness to our problems, a response to our questions, a broadening of our values and the fulfilment of our aspirations.[11]

---

10 St Thomas Aquinas, *Summa Theologiae*, Ia – IIae, q. 106, art 2.
11 Benedict XVI, *Verbum Domini*, 23.

As we listen to the word of God, the Holy Spirit will enlighten our minds and enable us to find, even in very dark or threatening moments, the presence of God. As the psalm says, "Hidden in the storm, I answered you" (Psalm 81:7). God remains hidden in the storms of our life but, without an active faith, we can easily feel that God has abandoned us in the storm.

## Fear is the big obstacle to listening

We have to discipline ourselves to listen to God's word in this way. The Lord is inviting us to enter into a dialogue with him about what is going on in our life. But we may be looking for a quick fix for our problems. God, however, never fails to help us if we are willing to receive the help God is offering. St Augustine understood this well when he wrote:

> Lord, that man is your best servant who is not so much concerned to hear from you what he wills as to will what he hears from you.[12]

God's constant word to us is, "Do not be afraid, for I have redeemed you; I have called you by your name, you are mine" (Isaiah 43:1). Fear is probably the one emotion that can prevent us from hearing what God is saying to us; not physical fear, which is a warning that there is danger around, but that pervasive fear about oneself, about not being "precious in God's sight" (see Isaiah 43:4), or the fear that paralyses our initiative in undertaking something new in case we will be criticised by others or in case we fail to succeed. Moses had that kind of fear when he said to God, "Who am I to go to Pharaoh?" God invited him to a deeper faith with the words, "I shall be with you" (Exodus 3:11-12). Moses had to learn through experience that God was with him in every situation, no matter how difficult or forbidding it may have been. We have to learn the same lesson: God is with us. It is only when we begin to truly trust the God who is always with us, that we can hear what God is saying

---

12 St Augustine, *Confessions*, 10. 26.

to us. As Benedict XVI said, "Scripture can only be understood if it is lived."[13] The more we try to live according to God's word, overcoming our fear, the more we begin to hear God's word and the more light the word begins to shine on all our experiences. As we sit at the "table of the word of God" we receive the reassurances that those disciples on the road to Emmaus received. Jesus wants to open the scriptures for us.

## From the table of the word of God to the table of the Body of the Lord

David Currie, who was, in his own words, born into a fundamentalist and anti-Catholic family in Texas, highlights how the Catholic Church in its worship now gives more time to the actual proclamation of the word of God than the other Christian traditions, especially those that claim that the Catholic Church is unbiblical. After many years of study and seeking, Currie, who had been ordained a minister in an evangelical church, set out to investigate the place that the word of God had in the worship of various churches in Chicago. He had devised this test. At a church service he would write down the length of time given to the actual proclamation of the word of God, then the time of the full service. He then divided the time given to the proclamation of the word into the total time of the service and he got the percentage of the service time given to the actual proclamation of the word. This is what he discovered:

> At an Evangelical church service 6% of worship time was given to the proclamation of the word of God.
> At a Fundamentalist church service 2% of worship time was given to the proclamation of the word of God.
> At a Catholic Mass on Sunday 26% of worship time was given to the proclamation of the word of God.[14]

---

13 Benedict XVI, *Verbum Domini*, 47.
14 David Currie, *Born Fundamentalist, Born Again Catholic* (San Francisco: Ignatius Press, 1996), p. 100.

We have three readings at the Sunday Mass. When the first reading is proclaimed well and the responsorial psalm well sung or proclaimed, and when the second reading is proclaimed with the same solemnity followed by the singing of the Gospel Acclamation and then the preparation for and solemn proclamation of the Gospel, at least ten or fifteen minutes will have transpired: a good twenty-six per cent of our average Mass time.

David Currie became a Catholic. He had set out to prove that the Catholic Church was unbiblical and he discovered in the very liturgy of the Mass that it is the Catholic Church that is truly the Church of the word of God. Catholics are well fed and nourished at the table of the word of God when they go to Mass. The proclamation of the word of God during Mass prepares us to take our place at the table of the Body of Christ. Benedict XVI wrote:

> "From the two tables of the word of God and the Body of Christ, the Church receives and gives to the faithful the bread of life." Consequently it must constantly be kept in mind that the word of God, read and proclaimed in the Church in the liturgy, leads to the Eucharist as to its own connatural end.[15]

Our fruitful participation in the Mass depends greatly on how we sit at the "table of the word of God", allowing the word to enlighten us. We have to listen in faith, hungry to hear the word of God. Every time we go to Mass we hear God's word to us about ourselves. We receive a revelation not only about God but also about ourselves. The Second Vatican Council made this very clear when it said:

> In reality it is only in the mystery of the Word made flesh that the mystery of humanity truly becomes clear. For Adam, the first man, was a type of him who was to come, Christ the Lord. Christ the new Adam, in the very

---

15 Benedict XVI, *Sacramentum Caritatis*, 44.

revelation of the mystery of the Father and of his love, fully reveals humanity to itself and brings to light its very high calling.[16]

Christ fully reveals us to ourselves. A very helpful spiritual exercise is to ask ourselves: "How does God really see us?" We don't have to guess at the answer because God has revealed to us exactly how God sees us. Just look at these words that God speaks to us about us:

- Made in the image and likeness of God (Genesis 1:27)
- Fallen and redeemed (Genesis 3; 2 Corinthians 5:17)
- Precious in God's sight (Isaiah 43:4)
- Little less than a god and crowned with glory and beauty (Psalm 8:5)
- Reborn of water and the Holy Spirit (John 3:5)
- God's temple (1 Corinthians 3:16)
- Temple of the Holy Spirit (1 Corinthians 6:19)
- God's work of art (Ephesians 2:10)
- The body of Christ (1 Corinthians 12:27).

When we take our place at the table of the word of God at Mass it is good to see ourselves as God sees us and not see ourselves through somebody's negative view of us. As the psalm says, "The Lord takes delight in his people" (Psalm 149:4). God wants us to feel very welcome at the table of God's word. The Lord has invited us to take our place at his table and he wants to speak to our hearts.

Both our origin and our destiny are mysteries hidden from us. God's word reveals both to us. Our origin is rooted in the profound mystery of God's choice of us. We are told that God "chose us in Christ before the world was made to be holy and faultless before him in love" (Ephesians 1:4). Our destiny is in the Lord's hands. Jesus says, "No one can come to me unless drawn by the Father who sent me, and I will raise that person up on the last day" (John

---

16 *Gaudium et Spes*, Pastoral Constitution on the Church in the Modern World, 22.

6:44). Jesus reveals to us the truth of our being: we come from God and we will return to God. This truth can only be received in faith. That is why we speak of "the light of faith". Without a light we can see nothing in the darkness. Some people draw the conclusion that because they can see nothing there is nothing to see. With the dawn of living faith the darkness is dispelled and we understand ourselves and our destiny in an entirely new way. At a Funeral Mass for a friend the family had chosen these words for the first reading: "Whether we live or whether we die we belong to the Lord" (Romans 14:8). Those words of revelation expressed the reality of faith that their father had lived. He believed with his whole heart the words of Jesus: "Anyone who does eat my flesh and drink my blood has eternal life, and I shall raise that person up on the last day" (John 6:54).

As we sit at the table of the word of God we learn the wonderful truth about ourselves, the amazing revelation that we will live for ever with God who forgives all our sins and who invites us to live in his love. We don't just think about these wonderful words of God but, as Jesus says, we live "on every word that comes from the mouth of God" (Matthew 4:4). This introduces us into a new spiritual depth of our being. If we live by God's word to us about ourselves we will refuse to listen to all the negative and discouraging words that are spoken to us: we allow God to tell us who we are in God's sight. As we live by God's word to us about ourselves, we begin to form our self-image. We begin to see ourselves as God sees us. We discover our true identity in God's word.

### The ministry of the word during Mass
Those who have the responsibility of proclaiming the scriptures during the Mass are asked to prepare themselves well. They are not just reading the words on a page. They are announcing a message from God. Before they can announce this message they must first hear it in their hearts. As Benedict XVI said:

> Only those who first place themselves in an attitude of listening to the word can go on to become its heralds.[17]

Without first hearing the word in our hearts it will be impossible for us to proclaim the word with conviction to the congregation. The ability to read well is a necessary gift for those chosen to proclaim the word of God during Mass. But even more important is the ability to prayerfully ponder the word in one's heart before going forward to proclaim it. Readers could develop this spiritual discipline as they prepare to announce the word: prayerfully reading over the passages several times during the week until they get a clear sense of the message they will be communicating; praying for the enlightenment of the Holy Spirit; pondering the word during the week in their hearts; when the time comes, proclaiming the word with confidence in the faith that it is through this proclamation that God speaks to God's people. As we begin to ponder the word, the simple question, "What is God saying to me in this reading?" helps to open the heart to this divine dimension of the word being proclaimed. As the Second Vatican Council said:

> In the sacred books the Father who is in heaven comes lovingly to meet his children, and talks with them.[18]

When we hear what the Father is saying to us we can then proclaim the passage well.

## Violence and immorality in the Bible

We encounter violence and immorality of all kinds in the Old Testament. The demands that such passages should be deleted have always been resisted by the Church on the grounds that revelation is deeply rooted in the history of God's people who had to struggle with all their human weaknesses in a fallen world. The Bible doesn't seek to cover up the wickedness that is often found in God's people. It doesn't whitewash the dark shadows that we find

---

17 Benedict XVI, *Verbum Domini*, 51.
18 *Dei Verbum*, 21.

even in Abraham and King David. The Gospels tell us quite bluntly about the betrayal of Judas and the denial of Peter. Such failures are the clearest sign that God's people need redemption. That is as true today of us as it was of the people before the time of Christ. When we hear the accounts of sinful actions in the Bible, like King David having Uriah, the husband of Bathsheba, killed to cover up his adultery (2 Samuel 11), we should not go into a judgemental pose. Rather, we should remember the times when we too failed to live the life of grace that God gave us at baptism. God is speaking to us now, not to David, because the word of God is alive and active. It is not spoken in the past. It is spoken to us in the present. The Bible makes it clear, in the words of St Paul, that "all have sinned" (Romans 3:23). Indeed, Paul boasts that he is the greatest sinner: "Christ Jesus came into the world to save sinners. I myself am the greatest of them" (1 Timothy 1:15).

There is no situation outside the love and mercy of God. There is no sin that God will not forgive once we turn to God for mercy. God is greater than our sins. But we have to remind ourselves, in the words of Benedict XVI:

> The root of sin lies in the refusal to hear the word of the Lord, and to accept in Jesus, the Word of God, the forgiveness which opens us to salvation.[19]

We can go through life acknowledging our sins of weakness, but maybe we never acknowledge our refusal to hear the word of God! If we approach the table of the word of God with this unrepentant sin in our hearts we will not hear the word of God. God will not speak to us if we don't want to listen! Then we will not be able to live "on every word that comes from the mouth of God" (Matthew 4:4). We will have deprived ourselves of the greatest blessing. Jesus says, "Blessed... are those who hear the word of God and keep it!"

---

19 Benedict XVI, *Verbum Domini*, 26.

(Luke 11:28). Jesus, because he has the word of eternal life, wants us to hear it, to live by it, to build our lives on it. He says,

> Everyone who listens to these words of mine and acts on them will be like a sensible man who built his house on rock. Rain came down, floods rose, gales blew and hurled themselves against that house, and it did not fall: it was founded on rock. But everyone who listens to these words of mine and does not act on them will be like a stupid man who built his house on sand. Rain came down, floods rose, gales blew and struck that house and it fell; and what a fall it had! (Matthew 7:24-27).

At each Mass, as we take our place at the table of the word of God, we need the grace and the enlightenment of the Holy Spirit to hear what the Lord has to say to us.

# Chapter Three

# Offering our gifts and ourselves to God

Before we move from the table of the word to take our place at the table of the Body of the Lord we have to first prepare our gifts and bring them to the altar. Our gifts are very simple: bread and wine. As they are being brought in procession to the altar a hymn is usually sung. The words of the hymn should keep our attention focused on what we are doing at this stage of the Mass.

Sometimes we might be thinking that we bring the bread and wine to the altar because the priest needs them for the consecration, when they will become the Body and Blood of Christ. While that is true, it is not the full truth. What is really happening is that we are now making a gift of ourselves to God. The bread and wine are the symbol of our self-offering. Our gifts of bread and wine represent ourselves. They take the place of ourselves. In bringing them to the altar we are saying, in effect, "With these gifts we offer you, God our Father, our very selves. As you accept our gifts, mercifully accept ourselves and as you transform our gifts, transform us too." It is very easy to overlook this fundamental meaning of bringing our gifts of bread and wine to the altar.

## The symbolic meaning of a gift

Gift-giving is one of the most beautiful human actions we can engage in. We all like to receive gifts for special times in our lives like birthdays or weddings or anniversaries. And we all like to give gifts. There is nothing more innate in the human heart than the urge to give a gift. But what are we trying to say when we give a friend or loved one a gift? Suppose it is your birthday and your best friend wants to give you a gift. He or she knows what you like. So your friend presents you with a beautiful bottle of wine. What is going on in that gift-giving? Is your friend saying, "It's your birthday, you love wine," or is your friend saying, "It's your birthday, I love you"? If the gift is not saying, "I love you," it is not a gift at all. It is an investment! Your friend will be having a birthday before too long.

Notice that there is a new dynamic created in the very act of gift-giving. Your friend is the *giver* of the gift to you and you become the *thanks-giver* to your friend for the beautiful gift, the symbol of love. You recognise in the gift a new expression of your friend's love. Indeed, in receiving the gift you are receiving the love of your friend, your friend's very self. And, as you gratefully receive the gift, your love is renewed and strengthened. That manifestation of true love brings peace and joy, healing and reconciliation. The same dynamic is at work when we give God our gift. We are the *giver* of the gift and God becomes *thanks-giver* to us for our gift. The bread and wine that we offer to God are received gratefully by God because they are the symbol of our love for God, the sign that we are now making a gift of ourselves to God in love and thanksgiving. The bread and wine represent "all that is within me" (Psalm 103:1); all the good and all the bad; all the light and all the darkness; all the virtue and all the vice; our whole being.

The offertory of the Mass can be a time of deep inner healing: our hurts and our inner wounds; our disappointment and our frustrations; our family upsets and our struggles with colleagues at work; our grief at the death of a loved one or the pain of a marriage break-up, all these fabrics of our lives we offer to God. At this stage of bringing our gifts to the altar it is important for us not to exclude any part of our lives, no matter how sinful something may have been. We have to offer to God everything about us. God knows everything and invites us to lovingly and trustingly offer

God everything. We see this in the way in which Jesus dined in the houses of those whom others considered to be public sinners. St Luke records the first such feasting with sinners in the household of a tax collector by the name of Levi. Jesus saw Levi "sitting by the customs house, and said to him, 'Follow me'. And leaving everything he got up and followed him" (Luke 5:27-28). Levi had become a disciple of Jesus. He had given up his former way of life and his former occupation as a tax collector. Now he wanted to honour the Lord who had given him this new life. St Luke says,

> Levi held a great reception in his house, and with them at table was a large gathering of tax collectors and others. The Pharisees and their scribes complained to his disciples and said, "Why do you eat and drink with tax collectors and sinners?" Jesus said to them in reply, "It is not those who are well who need the doctor, but the sick. I have not come to call the virtuous, but sinners to repentance" (Luke 5:29-32).

In the eyes of the Pharisees, a large group of tax collectors was the most disreputable group one could imagine. And there were Jesus and his disciples at table with them! But, we could ask, what were the complaining Pharisees doing at that party? Eugene LaVerdiere observes:

> This would suggest that in some or even many of the Lukan communities there were those who thought themselves righteous and who judged others as unrighteous. These Christian Pharisees were ready to be with Jesus and his disciples, but they objected to the presence of the tax collectors, whom they considered unrighteous.[1]

Even today a Pharisee or two might turn up at a Sunday Mass.

---

1  Eugene LaVardiere, *Dining in the Kingdom of God: The Origins of the Eucharist in the Gospel of Luke* (Chicago: Liturgical Training Publications, 1994), p. 43.

**Prayer of blessing**

All are welcome at the table of the Lord, because at his table the Lord receives our gifts and offers us in return the gift of himself. What we have to bring, then, to the table of the Lord is our sincere desire to be his disciples, just like Levi. As the priest receives our gifts of bread and wine, those symbols of ourselves, he blesses God for them. Holding up the bread he says:

> Blessed are you, Lord God of all creation,
> for through your goodness we have received
> the bread we offer you:
> fruit of the earth and work of human hands,
> it will become for us the bread of life.

The priest pours the wine that we have offered into the chalice and adds a drop of water, silently saying this remarkable prayer:

> By the mystery of this water and wine
> may we come to share in the divinity of Christ
> who humbled himself to share in our humanity.

In this prayer we are claiming our true identity and our true destiny. Now we are not just offering our gifts to God, we are asking that God gives us a share in the very divinity of Jesus. We have to ponder that request deeply. We believe that God is our loving creator. God made us in God's own image and likeness. We should be the visible manifestation of God in our world. But, alas, we have sinned. We need salvation. And so, in Mass, we acknowledge before God our sinfulness and open our hearts to receive God's mercy and forgiveness. That is why we are bringing our gifts to the altar. And, in the very act of gift-giving, the expression of our love of God, we are emboldened to make that extraordinary request: "may we come to share in the divinity of Christ". The reason we give for this bold request is: "Christ... humbled himself to share in our humanity." This wonderful request is made silently by the priest in our name. He prays, "may we come to share in the divinity of Christ". Often the people remain totally unaware that the priest is praying for this wonderful divinisation of their lives. We should remind ourselves frequently that the Mass is being offered for our divinisation, for our sharing in the divinity of Christ our Lord. What difference will it make to our way of living when we share in the divinity of Christ?

The priest then lifts up the chalice with the wine and the water and the request that we share in the divinity of Christ, and gives thanks to God:

> Blessed are you, Lord God of all creation,
> for through your goodness we have received
> the wine we offer you:
> fruit of the vine and work of human hands,
> it will become our spiritual drink.

We acknowledge in these blessings that the bread and wine we offer are God's gift to us, in the first place, and we recognise too that they come to us as the "fruit of the earth and work of human hands". Many people are involved in the process that delivers to us the bread and wine that we are offering: the farmers and the vineyard workers who till the soil, plant the seeds and care for the vines; the reapers who harvest the wheat crops and the grapes; those who mill the grains of wheat and bring the grapes to the wine press; those who bake the bread that we use at Mass and skilfully produce the wine from the fermenting grapes. A community of many workers, in different parts of the world, produce the bread and wine we bring to the altar. Our gifts are the work of all their hands and we praise God for them.

Our gifts of bread and wine, representing the gift that we are making of ourselves to God, are now placed on the altar. The only reason we are doing this is because Jesus, at the Last Supper, told us to do so in memory of him. Let us remind ourselves of what Jesus did during that Last Supper with the apostles. While celebrating the solemn Passover meal that commemorated the deliverance of the Jewish people from slavery in Egypt, Jesus took the bread and the wine and spoke the words that revealed a whole new dimension of our redemption and his abiding presence with us. Over the bread he said, "This is my body which will be given for you; do this as a memorial of me," and over the wine he said, "This cup is the new covenant in my blood which will be poured out for you" (Luke 22:19-20). Jesus said, "do this", do what I have done. It is because of his command that we have assembled and prayed, listened to the word of God and responded, brought our gifts and laid them on the altar. We are obeying the Lord's command and doing as he told us to do. The priest, acting now in the very person of Christ, extends his hands over our gifts on the altar and prays:

> Make holy, therefore, these gifts, we pray,
> by sending down your Spirit upon them like the dewfall,
> so that they may become for us
> the Body and Blood of our Lord Jesus Christ.[2]

### The first epiclesis: the invocation of the Spirit

All is now under the power and influence of the Holy Spirit. What is going to happen on the altar in the prayer of consecration will be the work of the Holy Spirit. Everything God does in the history of our salvation, God does through the Holy Spirit. God's great promise to God's people in the Old Testament was, "I shall pour out my spirit on all humanity" (Joel 3:1). God fulfilled that great promise and redeemed God's people through our Lord Jesus Christ. We remember how Christ came to be born into this world.

---

2  Eucharistic Prayer II.

The angel Gabriel said to Mary, Jesus' mother, "The Holy Spirit will come upon you… and the power of the Most High will cover you with its shadow" (Luke 1:35). The Son of God was conceived in Mary's womb and born into this world as our Lord and Saviour Jesus Christ. When that same Holy Spirit came on Jesus, after his baptism by John at the Jordan, he began his mission of preaching the Gospel. Because he began "with the power of the Spirit in him" (Luke 4:14), Jesus preached the good news of God's redeeming love; he healed those who were sick, and cast out evil spirits and raised the dead to life. It was through the Holy Spirit that Jesus "offered himself as the perfect sacrifice to God" on the cross for our salvation (Hebrews 9:14). Through the Holy Spirit, God raised the dead Jesus to the new life of the resurrection (Romans 8:11). Through the Holy Spirit, which Jesus poured out on his disciples at Pentecost, the Church of Christ came into existence. As the Second Vatican Council teaches:

> Rising from the dead… he sent his life-giving Spirit upon his disciples and through him set up his body which is the church as the universal sacrament of salvation.[3]

The Holy Spirit is involved in everything Jesus said and did. When Jesus said, "do this in memory of me", he knew that it would be through the Holy Spirit that his Church would be able to do it. That is why we invoke the Holy Spirit to come upon our gifts, just as the Spirit came on the Virgin Mary, just as the Spirit came on Jesus after his baptism, just as the Spirit came on the disciples after the ascension of Jesus. When the Spirit comes upon our gifts we can do what Jesus did.

**Jesus' promise**
Let us remind ourselves why Jesus did what he did at the Last Supper. In one of his great teachings in the synagogue in Capernaum, his local synagogue, Jesus said about himself,

---

3  *Lumen Gentium*, Dogmatic Constitution on the Church, 48.

> I am the living bread which has come down from heaven.
> Anyone who eats this bread will live for ever;
> and the bread that I shall give
> is my flesh, for the life of the world (John 6:51).

There were strong objections to what Jesus had said but he continued, with still greater emphasis,

> I tell you most solemnly,
> if you do not eat the flesh of the Son of Man
> and drink his blood,
> you will not have life in you.
> Anyone who does eat my flesh and drink my blood
> has eternal life,
> and I shall raise him up on the last day.
> For my flesh is real food
> and my blood is real drink.
> He who eats my flesh and drinks my blood
> lives in me
> and I live in him (John 6:53-56).

When they heard this amazing teaching of Jesus many of his disciples walked away, saying, "This is intolerable language. How could anyone accept it?" (John 6:60). Jesus didn't try to stop them leaving him. He didn't say, "I am just speaking symbolically," or "This is just a parable." Jesus went to great lengths to explain his parables to his disciples (see Matthew 13). Although Jesus knew that many of his disciples were shocked and dismayed at his teaching, he was not going to water it down. He meant what he said. In fact, he was quite prepared to let the twelve apostles go if they were not willing to accept his teaching. He turned to them and said, "What about you, do you want to go away too?" (John 6:67). Jesus was making it very clear that any disciple who was not prepared to accept what he had just said about the need to "eat my flesh and drink my blood" should depart. His whole mission hinged on what he said about being "the living bread which has come down from heaven", about what we call the Eucharist. Simon Peter answered, "Lord, who shall we go to? You have the message of eternal life, and we believe; we know that you are the Holy One of God" (John 6:68-69). Peter was the one who responded to Jesus when he asked the disciples, "But who do you say I am?" with the words, "You are the Christ... the Son of the living God" (Matthew 16:16). Now in this new situation when many of the disciples were deserting Jesus, Peter spoke up again and said, "You have the message of eternal life." Peter, the spokesman for the Twelve, was prepared to accept that what Jesus said about eating his body and drinking his blood was the message of eternal life and so he said, "we believe". He didn't say, "We understand, we know how you are going to fulfil this promise." He knew that what Jesus said could only be accepted in the faith that Jesus is "the Holy One of God".

Those disillusioned disciples who walked away were not present at the Last Supper when Jesus gave us himself as "the bread of life". As the Gospel records,

> When evening came he was at table with the twelve disciples... Now as they were eating, Jesus took some bread, and when he had said the blessing he broke it and gave it to the disciples. "Take it and eat," he said "this is my body." Then he took a cup, and when he had returned thanks he gave it to them. "Drink all of you from this," he said "for this is my blood, the blood of the covenant, which is to be poured out for many for the forgiveness of sins" (Matthew 26:20. 26-28).

Jesus was now fulfilling what he had said about being "the bread of life" in the synagogue in Capernaum. He was giving us his Body and Blood to eat and drink, not in their physical state but in their sacramental state. This is what he meant when he said, "I am the bread of life." We eat his Body and drink his Blood in the form of bread and wine. Through the power of the Holy Spirit, the Word became flesh. Now, through the power of that same Spirit, his flesh becomes bread, the bread of life. Contemplating this mystery, St Alphonsus Liguori exclaimed:

> If anything could shake my faith in the Eucharist it would not be the doubt as to how bread and wine could become flesh… because I should answer that God can do everything; but if I ask myself how could he love us so much as to make himself our food, I can only answer that this is a mystery of faith above my comprehension, and that the love of Jesus cannot be understood.[4]

Often non-Christians have accused Christians of practising a form of cannibalism because the only way they can visualise flesh and blood is in a physical way. We know that in celebrating the Mass we have entered into the mystery of God's redeeming love for us and that the living Lord Jesus, now seated at the right hand of the Father, gives us himself as the bread of life.

## Words of consecration

After invoking the Holy Spirit to come upon our gifts of bread and wine, the priest then proceeds and does exactly what Jesus did. He recalls the time and the setting of the Lord's words and action:

> At the time he was betrayed
> and entered willingly into his Passion,
> he took bread and, giving thanks, broke it,
> and gave it to his disciples, saying:
> Take this, all of you, and eat of it,
> for this is my Body,
> which will be given up for you.

---

4   St Alphonsus de Liguori, *The Holy Eucharist*, Centenary Edition, ed. E Grimm (New York: Benziger, 1887), p. 239.

In a similar way, when supper was ended,
he took the chalice
and, once more giving thanks,
he gave it to his disciples, saying:

Take this, all of you, and drink from it,
for this is the chalice of my Blood,
the Blood of the new and eternal covenant,
which will be poured out for you and for many
for the forgiveness of sins.[5]

### The mystery of faith

Then the priest proclaims, "The mystery of faith". What has
happened on the altar is not just one of the mysteries of our faith. It
is the mystery that sums up in itself everything that God has done
through Christ for our salvation. Christ our Saviour is truly present
on the altar, under the appearance of bread and wine, so that he can
fulfil his promise, "He who eats my flesh and drinks my blood lives
in me and I live in him" (John 6:56). We can now have the most
intimate communion with the Lord Jesus as we receive him in Holy
Communion, as our "bread of life", and as he answers our prayer to
become "sharers in his divinity". As St John Paul II said:

In the Eucharist we have Jesus, we have his redemptive
sacrifice, we have his resurrection, we have the gift of the
Holy Spirit, we have adoration, obedience and love of the
Father. Were we to disregard the Eucharist, how could we
overcome our own deficiency?[6]

We believe that, through the power of the Holy Spirit and the words
that Jesus speaks, our gifts of bread and wine become the Body and
Blood of Christ. The sacrifice of Christ for our salvation is now
sacramentally present on the altar. Jesus, "the bread come down
from heaven" (John 6:58), is with us, inviting us to "take and eat".

---

5  Eucharistic Prayer II.
6  John Paul II, *Ecclesia de Eucharistia*, 60.

St John Paul II said:

> When the Church celebrates the Eucharist, the memorial of her Lord's death and resurrection, this central event of salvation becomes really present and "the work of our redemption is carried out". This sacrifice is so decisive for the salvation of the human race that Jesus Christ offered it and returned to the Father only *after he had left us a means of sharing in it* as if we had been present there.[7]

But notice, it is not just any bread and wine that has been changed into Christ's Body. It is our gift, which represents us and everything about us that becomes for us the very Body and Blood of the Lord. When Jesus, through the Holy Spirit, transforms the bread and wine into his own Body and Blood he transforms us, too, and we become his body, we become "sharers in his divinity". St Paul says to us, "You together are Christ's body; but each of you is a different part of it" (1 Corinthians 12:27).

Our act of worship has now become Christ's act of worship of his Father in heaven. Fr Raymond Moloney writes:

> By the central action of Christ in the Mass, our worship is changed into the great mystery of worship which Christ himself offered on Calvary. But the same action requires that our offerings are changed into that which he offered on the cross, his own body and blood. As long as the offerings stand simply for our worship, it is enough if they remain simply bread and wine. But they cannot truly mean Christ's worship on the cross unless they become what he offered there, his own body and blood. Their new meaning requires the new reality.[8]

---

7  Ibid., 11.
8  Raymond Moloney SJ, *Our Splendid Eucharist* (Dublin: Veritas, 2003), p. 89.

**The second epiclesis on the community gathered**

Following the first epiclesis, the invocation of the Holy Spirit, and the consecration, when the bread and wine become the Body and Blood of Christ, the priest then invokes the Holy Spirit for a second time and asks that the Spirit may come on all present, with the words,

> grant that we, who are nourished
> by the Body and Blood of your Son
> and filled with his Holy Spirit,
> may become one body, one spirit in Christ.[9]

We have already prayed to be made "sharers in the divinity of Christ" and now we pray to be made "one body, one spirit in Christ". In the words of St Paul, we are "the body of Christ". Fr Raniero Cantalamessa explains it this way:

> There are two bodies of Christ on the altar: his *real* body (the body "born of the Virgin Mary", risen and ascended into heaven) and his *mystic* body, the Church. Thus, his real body is *really* present and his mystic body is *mystically* present, "mystically" meaning in virtue of its inseparable union with the Head. There is no confusion and no division between the two presences which are distinct.[10]

The mystery of faith, then, is twofold. The bread and wine are changed into the Body and Blood of Christ and we too are transformed and become "one body, one spirit in Christ". The Body of Christ becomes truly present under the appearance of the bread and wine on the altar and, at the same time, the body of Christ becomes mystically present in the disciples around the altar. That is the profound mystery of our faith involving both Christ and us. The *Catechism of the Catholic Church* teaches the depth of the mystery of faith by quoting the words of St Augustine:

---

9 Eucharistic Prayer III.
10 Raniero Cantalamessa, *The Eucharist* (Collegeville: Liturgical Press, 1995), p. 21.

> If you are the body and members of Christ, then it is your sacrament that is placed on the table of the Lord; it is your sacrament that you receive. To that which you are you respond, "Amen" ("yes, it is true!") and by responding to it you assent to it. For you hear the words, "the Body of Christ" and respond "Amen". Be then a member of the Body of Christ so that your *Amen* may be true.[11]

The Mass is the mystery not just of Christ becoming truly present in our gifts of bread and wine but also of Christ becoming mystically present in all of us sharing in the mystery of the Mass. The ultimate reason why Christ becomes truly present on the altar is because he yearns to be truly present in us, to make us "sharers in his divinity", to live his eternal life in and through us. As he said, "He who eats my flesh and drinks my blood lives in me and I live in him" (John 6:56). St Augustine was very aware that the mystery of us becoming the body of Christ can be overlooked. All our focus tends to be on Christ truly present under the appearance of bread and wine on the altar. It is easier, less challenging, to adore Christ at a distance, to keep him, as it were, on the altar. That can fill us with great devotion and reverence. It is much more challenging, however, to see Christ present in those who have gathered for the Mass, in "the sacred assembly" of the faithful, or to see him present in those who are poor, homeless or marginalised on the streets outside the church. That can make great demands on our generosity towards certain people and challenge us to let go of bad attitudes. St John Chrysostom, the great Archbishop of Constantinople (present-day Istanbul), said:

> You have tasted the Blood of the Lord, yet you do not recognise your brother... You dishonour this table when you do not judge worthy of sharing your food someone judged worthy to take part in this meal... God freed you

---

11 St Augustine, cited in the *Catechism of the Catholic Church*, 1396.

from all your sins and invited you here, but you have not become more merciful.[12]

## Becoming the Eucharist we celebrate

St John Chrysostom is saying that it is possible to come to the Eucharist without doing what Jesus did. When Jesus asked us to "do this in memory of me", what exactly was the "this" that he was referring to? Was he saying, "Just repeat the ritual that I have performed with the bread and wine"? Or was he saying, "Do the full meaning of what I have just done"? We find the same verbs used in all the accounts of what Jesus did at the Last Supper to bring out the full meaning of what he was doing: he took the bread, he blessed the bread, he broke the bread, and he shared the broken bread that had become his Body with his disciples. That action of breaking the bread was so significant in the early Christian community that the name given to the celebration of the Eucharist was "the breaking of the bread". We too break the "consecrated bread" at Mass, but we can easily forget that before the bread and wine became the Body and Blood of Christ on the altar they were the gifts that we offered to God, gifts symbolising the gift that we were making of ourselves to God. Now in "the breaking of the bread" it is ourselves, so often closed in on ourselves, that we have to break open and be willing to share as members of Christ. Fr Cantalamessa recounts how he began to see the Eucharist with new eyes when he realised that to do what Jesus did meant that he too had to "break" everything within himself that was not totally given to God and God's people:

> Then I understood that to "do" what Jesus did that night, I
> must, first of all, "break" myself and that is, lay before God
> all hardness, all rebellion towards him or towards others,
> crush my pride, submit and say "yes", fully, to all that God
> asks of me. I too must repeat the words, Lo, I have come to

---

12 St John Chrysostom, cited in the *Catechism of the Catholic Church*, 1397.

do thy will, O God! You don't want many things from me; you want me and I say "yes". To be Eucharist like Jesus signifies being totally abandoned to the Father's will.[13]

To do what Jesus did means that we must become the Eucharist we celebrate. We must break within ourselves the spirit of selfishness, meanness, arrogance, fault-finding and condemning of others. Then we can truly offer to others our service of love and acceptance, especially for those who are poor and rejected in our society. Mother Teresa believed that "our life must be woven with the Eucharist" and so she could say to her Sisters of Charity who were caring for the most abandoned poor people,

> Let the poor and the people eat you up… Let the people "bite" your smile, your time. You sometimes might prefer not to even look at somebody when you had some misunderstanding. Then, not only look, but give a smile… Learn by heart you must let the people eat you up.[14]

This is surely a very graphic description of how to become the Eucharist we celebrate. But that is what "going to Mass" involves. As we faithfully "go to Mass" and offer ourselves, with and through Christ, at the Eucharistic table, we are being progressively sanctified and divinised. As Benedict XVI said:

> The Eucharist, since it embraces the concrete, everyday existence of the believer, makes possible, day by day, the progressive transfiguration of all those called by grace to reflect the image of the Son of God.[15]

How can we grow in this appreciation of the mystery of the Mass and reverence the Body of Christ, not just on the altar, but in those who are around the altar, and those who are abandoned on our streets? St Augustine showed us the way:

---

13 Cantalamessa, *The Eucharist*, p. 18.
14 Brian Kolodiejchuk MC (ed.), *Come Be My Light: The Private Writings of the Saint of Calcutta* (New York: Doubleday, 2007), p. 285.
15 Benedict XVI, *Sacramentum Caritatis*, 71.

> The faithful will know the Body of Christ if they do not neglect to be the Body of Christ. Let them be the Body of Christ if they wish to live by the Spirit of Christ. Only the Body of Christ lives by the Spirit of Christ.[16]

Augustine is saying that if we want to really understand the mystery of the Mass, the holy Eucharist that we celebrate, we have to become Eucharist. We have to do what Jesus did. He took the bread and broke it and gave it to the disciples, saying, "This is my body given for you." He told us to do the same. Am I willing to "break the bread" of my life in a relationship where I haven't been giving my all in love and service? If I have been carrying a negative attitude towards somebody or harbouring unforgiveness or bitterness in my heart, am I willing to change? I will certainly not be able to change through my own strength. I will need the great miracle of redemption to be able to become the Eucharist I celebrate. St Alphonsus Liguori wrote:

> That as at the Eucharistic Table our Saviour offers us to eat and to drink his Body and Blood, we should also offer to him our body and blood by giving ourselves entirely to him, being ready to sacrifice our life for his glory, should it be necessary.[17]

To do what Jesus did, to become the Eucharist that we celebrate, to be the body of Christ, we humbly offer ourselves to the Father during Mass and open our hearts to be transformed by the Holy Spirit into the body of Christ for our brothers and sisters. That is what Jesus wants to do for us. As St Augustine imagined the Lord saying to us:

> I am the food of grown men; grow, and you shall feed upon me; nor shall you change me, like the food of the flesh, into yourself, but you shall be changed into me.[18]

16 St Augustine, *On The Gospel of John,* Tractate 26: 13, cited in James O'Connor, *The Hidden Manna* (San Francisco: Ignatius Press, 1988), p. 64.
17 St Alphonsus de Liguori, *The Holy Eucharist*, p. 35.
18 St Augustine, *Confessions*, 7. 10.

We pray for this transforming grace in each Mass as we say, "By the mystery of this water and wine may we come to share in the divinity of Christ who humbled himself to share in our humanity." "Going to Mass" in this spirit means being willing to become the Eucharist we celebrate.

# Chapter Four

## Until you come again

After the consecration the priest proclaims: "The mystery of faith". The Missal gives three possible acclamations by the people in response, of which the first is: "We proclaim your Death, O Lord, and profess your Resurrection until you come again." This response focuses our minds and hearts on the true nature of the mystery of our faith. It is the mystery of the life, death and resurrection of the Lord Jesus who is now present with us on the altar and who will come again in glory to judge the living and the dead. It is the mystery of "Jesus, who was *put to death for our sins* and raised to life to justify us" (Romans 4:25). The mystery of our faith is Christ's great work of our redemption through his death and resurrection. This great work is not a work that belongs to the past but a work that becomes present to us as we share in the Eucharist. The Second Vatican Council said:

> At the last supper, on the night he was betrayed, our Saviour instituted the eucharistic sacrifice of his body and blood. This he did in order to perpetuate the sacrifice of the cross throughout the ages until he should come again, and so to entrust to his beloved spouse, the church, a memorial of his death and resurrection: a sacrament of love, a sign of unity, a bond of charity, "a paschal banquet in which Christ is received, the mind is filled with grace, and a pledge of future glory is given to us."[1]

The Mass is the Lord's banquet, but a very specific kind of banquet. It is his sacrificial banquet which he shared with his apostles on the night before he was crucified. At this sacrificial banquet we share in both the sacrificial death and the glorious resurrection of Christ.

---

1 *Sacrosanctum Concilium*, Constitution on the Sacred Liturgy, 47.

St John Paul II wrote:

> This sacrifice is so decisive for the salvation of the human race that Jesus Christ offered it and returned to the Father only *after he had left us a means of sharing in it* as if we had been present there.[2]

When I first read that line in John Paul II's encyclical it resonated deeply with me and filled me with awe for the sacramental presence of the holy sacrifice of Christ's Body and Blood on the altar. What struck me in a new way was the phrase "as if we had been present there". I have used this phrase many times in my preaching and teaching on the Eucharist and each time it evokes in the hearers the same Eucharistic amazement that it first evoked in me. I always add the comment, "We are at no disadvantage because we were not present in the Upper Room in Jerusalem when Christ celebrated that first Mass. At our Sunday or daily Mass we are present at the same sacramental offering of himself that Jesus makes to the Father and shares with us as he says, 'This is my body given for you,' and 'This is my blood shed for you.'"

The Mass is not just a remembrance of a past event, the Last Supper; it is the sacramental presence of Christ's redemptive death and resurrection. We can now share in it "as if we had been present there". Because Christ's redemptive sacrifice is so essential for our salvation we had to have some tangible and visible way of being close to it, of feeling that it is happening for us in the present. That is why Jesus, knowing our human weakness, left us the Eucharist, the sacrament of his Body and Blood, so that we could share in it, just as the apostles shared in it on that first Holy Thursday evening. We are present at and sharing in the very same Eucharist that the Twelve shared in with Jesus each time we "go to Mass". We are seated with Jesus at the table of the Body of the Lord as he says to us, "Take and eat, this is my body" and "Take and drink, this is my

---

2   John Paul II, *Ecclesia de Eucharistia*, 11.

blood." We receive sacramentally the same Body and Blood of the Lord that the twelve apostles received at that first Mass. That truly is "the mystery of faith". As the Catechism says, "the Eucharist is the sum and the summary of our faith".[3] It is only in faith that we can "see" this mystery. St Thomas Aquinas, the greatest theologian of the Church, turned to poetry to express this great truth. He wrote:

> Godhead here in hiding, whom I do adore
> Masked by these bare shadows, shape and nothing more,
> See, Lord, at thy service low lies here a heart
> Lost, all lost in wonder at the God thou art.
>
> Seeing, touching, tasting are in thee deceived;
> How says trusty hearing? That shall be believed;
> What God's Son has told me, take for truth I do;
> Truth himself speaks truly or there's nothing true.[4]

As we bow in adoration before Christ truly present on the altar we are opening our hearts to receive the full forgiveness of all our sins, which is the grace and the fruit of his great sacrifice. The work of our redemption is being accomplished as we receive the "bread of life" and share in the mystery of the Mass. To everyone who shares our faith in the Mass, Jesus our resurrected Lord, seated at the right hand of the Father, says, "Take and eat, this is my body; take and drink, this is my blood." It is the living Lord Jesus, present in our midst, who invites us to share in the Eucharistic banquet. And this is not a remembrance of a past event but a participation in a present reality. As St John Paul II said,

> In this gift [of the Eucharist] Jesus Christ entrusted to his Church the perennial making present of the paschal mystery.[5]

---

3  *Catechism of the Catholic Church*, 1327.
4  As cited in *Catechism of the Catholic Church*, 1381.
5  John Paul II, *Ecclesia de Eucharistia*, 5.

## Paschal mystery

The phrase "paschal mystery" needs a few words of explanation. It has its origin in the Jewish feast of Passover (*Pesach* in Hebrew) which commemorates the deliverance of God's people from slavery in Egypt. The angel of God passed over the Israelite homes that had their lintels and doorposts marked with the blood of a lamb slain for the occasion (Exodus 12:21-24). Ever since then the Jews have celebrated their Passover and share a "paschal meal" by eating "the paschal lamb". The paschal lamb, symbol of their deliverance from Egypt, prefigured the one whom St John the Baptist called "the lamb of God that takes away the sin of the world" (John 1:29). It was while Jesus was gathered with the apostles to eat the Passover meal that he gave this solemn religious commemoration, sacred to God's people of the old covenant, a whole new meaning when he took the bread and said, "This is my body given for you; do this in remembrance of me." Then he took the cup filled with wine and said, "This cup is the new covenant in my blood poured out for you" (Luke 22:19-20).The Mass is our celebration of the new covenant, of the "paschal mystery", of our redemption from sin, through the passion, death, resurrection and ascension into heaven of our Saviour Jesus Christ. As Benedict XVI wrote:

> The institution of the Eucharist demonstrates how Jesus' death, for all its violence and absurdity, became in him a supreme act of love and mankind's definitive deliverance from evil.[6]

## The sacrifice of Christ

The Mass makes sacramentally present to us, under the appearance of bread and wine, the paschal mystery, the redeeming sacrifice that Christ offered to the Father on our behalf. Sacrifice is the manifestation of self-giving love. Christ's sacrifice of his life was the gift of himself that he made in love to his Father. That gift of self

---

6  Benedict XVI, *Sacramentum Caritatis*, 10.

cost him his life in this world because his enemies were determined to kill him. But it was not the bloody crucifixion by itself that was the sacrifice. Many others at the time of Jesus were crucified for rebelling against Roman imperial power and their deaths were not sacrifices. Christ's death was a sacrifice because it was a total gift of himself, freely given to God the Father, on our behalf. As Jesus said, "No one can have greater love than to lay down his life for his friends" (John 15:13). It was with this great love for us in his heart that Jesus began to share the Passover meal with his disciples. St Luke tells us,

> When the time came he took his place at table, and the apostles with him. And he said to them, "I have longed to eat this Passover with you before I suffer; because, I tell you, I shall not eat it again until it is fulfilled in the kingdom of God" (Luke 22:14-16).

Jesus was longing to show the apostles his unconditional and limitless love for the Father and for us. It was this love that would take him from the Upper Room in Jerusalem, where he gave us the Eucharist, to the hill of Calvary, where he died for us. As Brant Pitre points out,

> By means of the Last Supper, Jesus transformed the Cross into a Passover, and by means of the Cross, he transformed the Last Supper into a sacrifice.[7]

His agonising death on the cross did not bring that eternal love in the heart of Jesus to an end. God the Father raised him to the new life of the resurrection in the Holy Spirit and seated him at his right hand in glory. From there he poured out on us the Holy Spirit.

Through the Holy Spirit we have become the body of Christ. It is as his mystical body on earth that we gather to celebrate his paschal mystery: his death, resurrection, ascension into heaven and the

---

7  Brant Pitre, *Jesus and the Jewish Roots of the Eucharist* (New York: Doubleday, 2011), p. 169.

pouring out on us of the Holy Spirit. It is the sending of the Holy Spirit that creates the Church. As the Second Vatican Council said:

> By communicating his Spirit, Christ mystically constitutes as his body his brothers and sisters who are called together from every nation.[8]

The Council specifically draws attention to the centrality of the resurrection of Christ, the coming of the Spirit and the creation of the Church with this teaching:

> Rising from the dead... he sent his life-giving Spirit upon his disciples and through him set up his body which is the church as the universal sacrament of salvation.[9]

When we profess the Lord's resurrection we are confessing our faith in the power of the Holy Spirit who raised him from the dead and who formed out of us, his brothers and sisters, his mystical body, his Church on earth. This is the mystery of faith: Christ in his risen and glorified body on the altar and we the mystical body of Christ around the altar, and in all parts of the world, celebrating the Mass and looking forward to the Lord's return in glory.

When we respond with the words, "We proclaim your Death, O Lord, and profess your Resurrection," we are confessing that:

> The Eucharistic Sacrifice makes present not only the mystery of the Saviour's passion and death, but also the mystery of the resurrection which crowned his sacrifice.[10]

Jesus died in his mortal body and was raised with an immortal, totally divinised body in the resurrection. It is this divinised, glorified and immortal body that becomes sacramentally present under the appearance of bread and wine during Mass. St John Paul II writes:

---

8  *Lumen Gentium*, Dogmatic Constitution on the Church, 7.
9  Ibid., 48.
10 John Paul II, *Ecclesia de Eucharistia*, 14.

The sacramental re-presentation of Christ's sacrifice, crowned by the resurrection, in the Mass involves a most special presence which – in the words of Paul VI – "is called 'real' not as a way of excluding all other types of presence as if they were 'not real', but because it is a presence in the fullest sense: a substantial presence whereby Christ, the God-Man, is wholly and entirely present".[11]

This is why Catholics hold the Mass in such reverence. Even if we cannot explain very well the great truths that we believe about the Mass, we know that we believe them. Christ is truly present in his risen and glorified body, sharing with us the gift of the Holy Spirit, the pledge of our own resurrection from the dead. That is the mystery of faith. And it is only through the gift of faith that we can believe. Without that gift of faith no one can believe what we believe about Jesus being truly present on the altar during Mass.

**The second coming of Christ**

Our proclamation, "We proclaim your Death, O Lord, and profess your Resurrection until you come again", reminds us of that other great truth of our faith, namely, the second coming of Christ. Jesus said, "When the Son of Man comes in his glory, escorted by all the angels, then he will take his seat on his throne of glory" (Matthew 25:31). We profess in our Creed during Mass, "He will come again in glory to judge the living and the dead." In every Mass we remind ourselves of this final fulfilment of God's plan for our redemption. In the great prayer for deliverance from all evil, after the Lord's Prayer, we say that "we await the blessed hope and the coming of our Saviour, Jesus Christ". In the Eucharistic Prayers of the Mass we pray:

> Therefore, O Lord, as we celebrate the memorial
> of the saving Passion of your Son,
> his wondrous Resurrection

---

11 John Paul II, *Ecclesia de Eucharistia*, 15.

and Ascension into heaven,
and as we look forward to his second coming...[12]

Therefore, O Lord,
as we now celebrate the memorial of our redemption,
we remember Christ's Death
and his descent to the realm of the dead,
we proclaim his Resurrection
and his Ascension to your right hand,
and as we await his coming in glory,
we offer you his Body and Blood,
the sacrifice acceptable to you
which brings salvation to the whole world.[13]

If we wish to truly "attune our minds to our voices"[14] in the Mass we begin to consciously make this longing for the second coming of Christ, expressed in these prayers, our own. We are waiting for the fulfilment of the final stage of our redemption when Christ will come again in glory. In faith, we acknowledge that he is sacramentally present, body and blood, soul and divinity on the altar under the appearance of bread and wine. When he comes again we will see him in all his glory. We shall become like him. St John says,

We are already the children of God
but what we are to be in the future has not yet been revealed;
all we know is, that when it is revealed
we shall be like him
because we shall see him as he really is (1 John 3:2).

When Christ comes again we shall see him in his resurrected state because we too will have been resurrected from the dead. As we profess in our Creed: "I look forward to the resurrection of the dead and the life of the world to come."

---

12 Eucharistic Prayer III.
13 Eucharistic Prayer IV.
14 See *Sacrosanctum Concilium*, 11.

## Our resurrection from the dead

In his response to the Sadducees who didn't believe in the resurrection Jesus reminded them that "At the resurrection men and women do not marry; no, they are like the angels in heaven" (Matthew 22:30). In the resurrection we will be *like* angels, we will not *be* angels. Our human nature will remain the same, but by our becoming *like* angels a new spiritualisation will have occurred. Resurrection will mean the restoration of bodiliness. The human person is an embodied being, not a pure spirit. We cannot speculate about what kind of a body the resurrected body will be. God has not revealed that to us. This doesn't mean, however, that we can't contemplate this final reality of our existence, namely, our being raised to the new life of the resurrection in the glory of God. That is our ultimate destiny for which, deep down, we are all yearning. As St Augustine said, "You have made us for yourself, O Lord, and our hearts will find no peace until they rest in you."[15] All the joys of this life are but a foretaste of the joy to come. God created us, not for everlasting life in this world, but to be eternally with God in the world to come. To enter into this new and everlasting life we need the transformation and the spiritualisation of the resurrection.

In the resurrection, our human bodies will not simply be spiritualised, they will be fundamentally divinised. This is what we pray for in every Mass. As the priest adds water to the wine, he prays,

> By the mystery of this water and wine
> may we come to share in the divinity of Christ
> who humbled himself to share in our humanity.

God's purpose for us and for our world will be achieved and God's image and likeness will become visible in us when we fully share in the divinity of Christ. We will share fully in Christ's resurrected

---

15 St Augustine, *Confessions*, 1. 1.

life. St John Paul II explored our resurrection and our divinisation at great depth. He wrote:

> Participation in the divine nature, participation in the inner life of God himself, penetration and permeation of what is essentially human by what is essentially divine, will then reach its peak, so that the life of the human spirit will reach a fullness that was absolutely inaccessible to it before. This new spiritualisation will be the *fruit of grace*, that is, *of God's self-communication in his very divinity*, not only to the soul, but *to the whole of man's psychosomatic subjectivity*.[16]

But our spiritualised bodies will remain totally human. A disincarnated body would be a dehumanised body. What we see in Christ's resurrected body is the human body completely integrated into the new life of the resurrection. As St John Paul II wrote:

> *Spiritualisation* signifies not only that the spirit will master the body, but, I would say, that *it will also fully permeate the body and the powers of the spirit will permeate the energies of the body*.[17]

We shall become like Christ when he returns in glory. That is why we yearn for it in every Mass. We say we are waiting for it, longing for his second coming. Then, in heaven, in the beatific vision, we will see God face to face. God, in the total mystery of being Father, Son and Holy Spirit, will communicate himself to each one of us, both individually and as a communion of saints. It will be that communion which will constitute the beatific state, the state of complete human fulfilment. As the Catechism says:

> It will be the definitive realisation of God's plan to bring under a single head "all things in [Christ], things in heaven and things on earth".[18]

---

16 John Paul II, *Theology of the Body* (Boston: Pauline Press, 2006), 67. 3.
17 Ibid.
18 *Catechism of the Catholic Church*, 1043.

When we say that we are looking forward to Christ's return we are also saying that we are looking forward to the fulfilment of this glorious plan that God has for each of us. We should put our hearts into that proclamation during Mass that "he will come again". But in our weak, sinful condition, we know our need of God's redeeming grace and we experience a daily struggle to live by that grace. St John Paul II encourages us with these words:

> Proclaiming the death of the Lord "until he comes" (1 Corinthians 11:26) entails that all who take part in the Eucharist be committed to changing their lives and making them in a certain way completely "Eucharistic". It is the fruit of a transfigured existence and a commitment to transforming the world in accordance with the Gospel which splendidly illustrates the eschatological tension inherent in the celebration of the Eucharist and in the Christ life as a whole: "Come, Lord Jesus!"[19]

**Eschatological tension**

By "eschatological tension" St John Paul II is referring to our state of waiting: we have been redeemed but our redemption will not be fully manifest until we are raised from the dead at the second coming of Christ. The word "eschatological" comes from the Greek word *eschatos*, which means the "last" – the last things in human destiny, which are death, judgement, heaven or hell. The branch of theology that studies "the last things" is called "eschatology". When St John Paul II speaks about "eschatological tension" he is referring to the struggle we all experience between our baptism, when we were reborn of water and the Holy Spirit, and our death, when we will arrive at the mercy seat of God our Father.

We believe in our redemption and we celebrate it every time we participate in Mass. But we also experience sinfulness and

---

19 John Paul II, *Ecclesia de Eucharistia*, 20.

weakness as we make our pilgrim journey back to the Father. We all sin, but Christ offers each of us the grace to repent of our sins. It is unrepentant sin that is the great danger on our journey back to God. We can experience great darkness and maybe at times feel that God has abandoned us. We have to live by faith, not by sight or feeling. That is the eschatological tension. We are waiting in hope. As St Paul said,

> You are waiting for our Lord Jesus Christ to be revealed; and he will keep you steady and without blame until the last day, the day of our Lord Jesus Christ, because God by calling you has joined you to his Son, Jesus Christ; and God is faithful (1 Corinthians 1:7-9).

### The last judgement

We profess in our Creed that Christ "will come again in glory to judge the living and the dead". The time of his second coming will be the time of the last judgement on the whole human race. Those who have chosen to do good in this life will pass with Christ into the glory of God, while those who have chosen to do only evil, and remained unrepentant in their evil choice, will be banished to the outer darkness. Jesus speaks very graphically about the last judgement:

> When the Son of Man comes in his glory, escorted by all the angels, then he will take his seat on his throne of glory. All the nations will be assembled before him and he will separate men one from another as the shepherd separates sheep from goats. He will place the sheep on his right hand and the goats on his left (Matthew 25:31-33).

The judgement will be about what we have done or failed to do for others in need. To those who were kind and generous to the needy, Jesus will say,

> Come you whom my Father has blessed, take for your heritage the kingdom prepared for you since the foundation of the world… in so far as you did this to one of the least of these brothers of mine, you did it to me (Matthew 25:34-40).

And to those who closed their hearts against those in need, Jesus will say,

> Go away from me, with your curse upon you, to the eternal fire prepared for the devil and his angels… in so far as you neglected to do this to one of the least of these, you neglected to do it to me (Matthew 25:41-46).

As we profess that Christ will come again we are reminding ourselves that when he comes in glory he will be our judge. He will be asking us how we have lived the Eucharist we have celebrated. Have I lived in communion with my brothers and sisters? As Benedict XVI pointed out:

> The Eucharist is the sacrament of communion between brothers and sisters who allow themselves to be reconciled in Christ, who made of Jews and pagans one people, tearing down the wall of hostility which divided them (cf. Ephesians 2:14). Only this constant impulse towards reconciliation enables us to partake worthily of the Body and Blood of Christ (cf. Matthew 5:23-24).[20]

In this time of grace he is our saviour, our redeemer who died for our salvation. But at the end of time, when he comes again, it will be, as the Creed says, "to judge the living and the dead".

In this time of grace we can live with "this constant impulse towards reconciliation"; we have received the gift of our salvation; we have not yet arrived at our eternal home in the kingdom of God; we are pilgrims in this world making our way to our eternal home

---

20 Benedict XVI, *Sacramentum Caritatis*, 89.

in heaven. When Christ comes again the salvation of the whole world will be achieved. St Paul says,

> Christ has in fact been raised from the dead, the first-fruits of all who have fallen asleep. Death came through one man and in the same way the resurrection of the dead has come through one man. Just as all men die in Adam, so all men will be brought to life in Christ; but all of them in their proper order: Christ as the first-fruits and then, after the coming of Christ, those who belong to him. After that will come the end, when he hands over the kingdom to God the Father (1 Corinthians 15:20-24).

We are waiting for that glorious return of the Lord when the salvation of the whole world will be achieved.

When we respond with the acclamation "We proclaim your Death, O Lord, and profess your Resurrection, until you come again", we are praying for Christ's coming in glory. In fact, we are saying, "Until you come again we will continue do what we are doing, namely, proclaiming your death and resurrection in the celebration of the Mass." As Cardinal Schönborn says:

> We ought to be more conscious, when we celebrate the Mass, that the liturgy not only makes the Lord present but also longs for his future coming.[21]

And he points out that,

> This yearning for the return of the Lord is the driving force in the liturgy. Is it this same yearning that moves us to take part in the liturgy?[22]

How consciously are we yearning for Christ's return in glory when we say, "until you come again"? How do we "attune our minds to our voices" as we say that prayer? We know that the return of

---

21 Christoph Cardinal Schönborn, *The Source of Life: Exploring the Mystery of the Eucharist* (San Francisco: Ignatius Press, 2007), p. 50.
22 Ibid.

Christ in glory will be the end of this world as we know it. People often refer to the "*end* of the world" as if it will be the greatest catastrophe to befall the human race. Our world has an end, that is, it has a purpose for its existence. When that purpose for which God created the world has been achieved, then its end will be reached. Far from being a calamity, something to be dreaded, the end of the world will coincide with the great return of Christ in glory. St Peter says, "What we are waiting for is what he promised: the new heavens and new earth, the place where righteousness will be at home" (2 Peter 3:13). In each Mass we look forward to this end, to the world being completely redeemed according to the original plan of God when, as St Paul says, "God may be all in all" (1 Corinthians 15:28).

### The seed of living hope

Our proclamation, "We proclaim your Death, O Lord, and profess your Resurrection until you come again", opens our hearts to be filled with joyful hope as "we await… the coming of our Saviour, Jesus Christ". The Mass activates this joyful hope in our hearts and gives us the confidence and courage to share our hope for humanity with everyone. The Second Vatican Council said:

> One is right in thinking that the future of humanity rests with people who are capable of providing the generations to come with reasons for living and for hope.[23]

Who has better reasons for hoping than those who believe that Christ will come again in glory? But before we can give people the reason for living and hoping we have to keep that hope alive in our own hearts. The source of that hope is in our Sunday or daily Eucharist. As St John Paul II said:

> [The Eucharist] spurs us on our journey through history and plants a seed of living hope in our daily commitment to the work before us. Certainly the Christian vision leads

---

23 *Gaudium et Spes*, Pastoral Constitution on the Church in the Modern World, 31.

to the expectation of "new heavens" and "a new earth" (Revelation 21:1) but this increases, rather than lessens, *our sense of responsibility for the world today.*[24]

Men and women of faith have always led the struggle for justice, human rights and human dignity. Their waiting in joyful hope for the coming of Christ in glory has filled them with evangelical passion and courage in the face of injustice. This evangelical passion is, as St John Paul II said:

> [The] fruit of a transfigured existence and a commitment to transforming the world in accordance with the Gospel.[25]

In 1980 the great martyr Archbishop Oscar Romero of San Salvador was shot while celebrating Mass for his oppressed people because he had become the "voice of the voiceless" and embodied in himself his people's struggle for justice. Romero was a man of Eucharistic hope. As Pope Francis says:

> True Christian hope, which seeks the eschatological kingdom, always generates history... The Church "cannot and must not remain on the sidelines in the fight for justice".[26]

Faith like Romero's truly generates history and shows us how hoping for the return of Christ in glory becomes the compelling motive for the Church's involvement in the struggle for justice in our world. Evil will not win the final victory. Christ, in dying for us and in giving us the Eucharist, has delivered humankind from definitive evil. As Benedict XVI pointed out:

> The institution of the Eucharist demonstrates how Jesus' death, for all its violence and absurdity, became in him a supreme act of love and mankind's definitive deliverance from evil.[27]

---

24 John Paul II, *Ecclesia de Eucharistia*, 20.
25 Ibid.
26 Pope Francis, *Evangelii Gaudium*, 181, 183.
27 Benedict XVI, *Sacramentum Caritatis*, 10.

Martyrs like Romero testify to the power of the Eucharist in facing evil situations in this life. In communion with all our great martyr saints we too can look forward to the future with great confidence because we believe in our "definitive deliverance from evil". Evil will not triumph.

Jesus promised, "the gates of the underworld can never overpower [the Church]" (Matthew 16:18). In the Mass we are grateful not just for the present but also for the future. Our gift of joyful hope is the virtue that enables us to reach out and lay hold of tomorrow and to declare in advance that tomorrow will be good, for tomorrow will come to us from God. The future will come to us as a gift from our heavenly Father. In the Mass we receive the grace to banish all anxiety about the future as we live the joyful hope that enables us to look forward to "the coming of our Saviour, Jesus Christ". The Mass provides us with the wonderful sacramental moment when we can say to Jesus on the altar, "until you come again" and "Come, Lord Jesus!"

Sometimes I think that we can allow the gift of joyful hope to remain inactive in our lives. If we had only ourselves to rely on it would be natural to be anxious and fearful about the future. But in the Mass we welcome Christ as our Saviour and we welcome one another as members of Christ's body. We are never all alone and we never have to rely on ourselves alone for our salvation. Christ alone is our Saviour and, even in all the trials and uncertainties of our situation, we have his great, victorious return in glory to look forward to. Neglect of this wonderful truth of our faith would rob us of great consolation in the present, especially when things are going wrong and when troubles mount up.

Our proclamation "until you come again" puts all our troubles into perspective. The present may be difficult, but our future is absolutely certain. The salvation that we celebrate in the Mass is the guarantee of our future. But we have to receive this guarantee in faith. As scripture says, "Only faith can guarantee the blessings that we hope for, or prove the existence of the realities that at present remain unseen" (Hebrews 11:1). The fact that the blessings we are hoping for remain unseen and unfelt is no reason for not reaching out in joyful hope and claiming them. Christ's victory over sin and death is real. We celebrate that victory in every Mass. Therefore, when we say that we are waiting in joyful hope "for the coming of our Saviour" we should invite the Holy Spirit to inject joy into our expectation. If we hold on instead to a pessimistic outlook, if we allow our attitudes to be infected with negativity about life, if we continue to criticise and find fault with everyone around us, we make it impossible to be filled with joyful hope.

In the Mass we are invited to cultivate hope rather than pessimism; to proclaim Christ's return in glory rather than indulge in despair about the world; to rejoice in the resurrection of Jesus from the dead and deepen our faith in our own resurrection. Death, then, loses its power to hold us in fear. As St Paul says,

> When this perishable nature has put on imperishability, and when this mortal nature has put on immortality, then the words of scripture will come true: *Death is swallowed up in victory. Death, where is your* victory? *Death, where is your sting?* Now the sting of death is sin... So let us thank God for giving us the victory through our Lord Jesus Christ (1 Corinthians 15:54-57).

It is with our hearts uplifted, and not just with our lips, that we respond, "We proclaim your Death, O Lord, and profess your Resurrection until you come again." That is how we see our life. Christ will come again. That is the ultimate source of our joy and confidence because, as St John says,

We are already the children of God
but what we are to be in the future has not yet been revealed;
all we know is, that when it is revealed
we shall be like him
because we shall see him as he really is (1 John 3:2).

# Chapter Five

# Holy Communion: receiving and being received by Christ

The Eucharistic Prayer of the Mass concludes with the priest holding up the sacrament of the Body and Blood of Christ and proclaiming: "Through him, and with him and in him, O God, almighty Father, in the unity of the Holy Spirit, all glory and honour is yours, for ever and ever." In this prayer, known technically as the doxology, Christ, in the person of the priest, offers the sacrifice of his Body and Blood to the Father and invites us to offer ourselves in thanksgiving to the Father. St Augustine said, "If you are the body and members of Christ, then it is your sacrament that is placed on the table of the Lord; it is your sacrament that you receive."[1] We have become the body of Christ which we are now offering to the Father in the doxology. Together, as the body of Christ, the whole congregation responds to the priest's proclamation with a loud "Amen". This is known as "the great Amen". With this ancient Hebrew word we are saying our "Yes" to what the priest has just said; "Yes" to the offering of ourselves to God; "Yes" to the mystery that here and now we stand with Christ in God's presence as the body of Christ; "Yes" to the wonderful truth that through Christ we offer the almighty Father all glory and honour. We can give no greater honour to God than what we are giving to God at that very moment. So we should put our hearts into shouting out our "Amen".

## The Lord's Prayer
The Communion Rite of the Mass begins with the words, "At the Saviour's command and formed by divine teaching we dare to say". The congregation is invited to stand and as one family,

---

1 Cited in *Catechism of the Catholic Church*, 1396.

one people of God, say together the Lord's Prayer. We say to God that we are one and so we can call God "Our Father", not just my Father, or your Father, but "Our Father". We are acknowledging that we are brothers and sisters because those who have a common father are brothers and sisters. As Benedict XVI said, "The Our Father overcomes all boundaries and makes us one family."[2]

In preparation for Holy Communion we ask God our Father to dismantle all barriers that obstruct our unity, by forgiving us our sins, just as we forgive those who sin against us. Before we ask for this great grace of forgiveness we ask the Father to "give us this day our daily bread". What are we asking for when we ask for "our daily bread"? In this petition we are not just asking God for a loaf or a cake of bread. The word translated "daily", from the original Greek text of the Our Father in the New Testament, is *epiousios*. This is the only occasion when this word appears in the scriptures. The great theologian Origen (died c. AD 254), one of the greatest Greek scholars, said that "*epiousios* does not appear anywhere else in Greek, but that it was coined by the Evangelists".[3] For St Jerome, who translated the Hebrew and Greek Old and New Testaments into Latin, *epiousios* should be translated as our "supersubstantial bread", our supernatural bread, our Eucharistic bread. Benedict XVI said:

> The Fathers of the Church were practically unanimous in understanding the fourth petition of the Our Father (for our daily bread) as a eucharistic petition; in this sense the Our Father figures in the Mass liturgy as a eucharistic table-prayer (i.e., "grace").[4]

Clearly we have lost a lot of the original meaning of "give us this day our daily bread", our *epiousios* bread, or our "supersubstantial" bread. We are asking the Father for supernatural bread, the bread of life. The *Catechism of the Catholic Church* helps us to reclaim the original meaning of the phrase:

---

2  Benedict XVI, *Jesus of Nazareth* (London: Bloomsbury, 2007), p. 141.

3  Ibid., p. 153.

4  Ibid., p. 154.

"Daily" (*epiousios*) occurs nowhere else in the New Testament. Taken in a temporal sense, this word is a pedagogical repetition of "this day" to confirm us in trust "without reservation". Taken in the qualitative sense, it signifies what is necessary for life, and more broadly every good thing sufficient for subsistence. Taken literally (*epiousios*: "super-essential"), it refers directly to the Bread of Life, the Body of Christ, the "medicine of immortality", without which we have no life within us. Finally in this connection, its heavenly meaning is evident: "this day" is the Day of the Lord, the day of the feast of the kingdom, anticipated in the Eucharist that is already the foretaste of the kingdom to come. For this reason it is fitting for the Eucharistic liturgy to be celebrated each day.[5]

The Our Father is our "grace" before we share the heavenly banquet of Holy Communion.

## Forgive us as we forgive them

As we stand before God, acknowledging him as our Father and acknowledging ourselves as God's sons and daughters, we ask, in the very first place, for our Eucharistic bread, the bread of life, and we ask for the forgiveness of our sins. But we make our forgiveness of others the measure of the forgiveness that we want to receive from God. We say, "forgive us... as we forgive". That can be a very challenging prayer to say, especially if we are going through a difficult time with someone. We must include everyone in that "our" of the "Our Father". Even our greatest enemy, and all the people who may not like us or those whom we may not like, all are included as we stand and address God as "Our Father". We cannot partake of the "one bread" of the Eucharist if we are not one. St Paul puts this great truth quite clearly: "The fact that there is only one loaf means that, though there are many of us, we form a single

---

5 *Catechism of the Catholic Church*, 2837.

body because we all have a share in this one loaf" (1 Corinthians 10:17). It is as a "single body", the body of Christ, that we share the "one bread".

We will not receive God's forgiveness if we do not forgive others. If there is one person whom I am not forgiving from my heart, at this stage of the Mass, I am resisting becoming "one body, one spirit in Christ". We cannot be complacent about this. Jesus says quite strongly, "Yes, if you forgive others their failings, your heavenly Father will forgive you yours; but if you do not forgive others, your Father will not forgive your failings either" (Matthew 6:14-15).

## Living in communion

I will not be able to have a loving relationship with God while harbouring an unloving attitude towards a brother or sister. Loving doesn't imply liking. Jesus said to us, "Love your enemies and pray for those who persecute you" (Matthew 5:44). We are not expected to like the enemy but we are expected, as Christ's disciples, to pray for him or her. Being able to ask God to bless enemies is the sign that we love them, that we do wish them well, that we do not wish some evil to befall them. We can then be at peace and share in the celebration of the Mass even with our enemies in the congregation.

Our relationship with others manifests the quality of our relationship with God. If we are in a loving relationship of union and communion with God, this relationship will be embodied and made manifest in our relationships with our sisters and brothers. Within the Christian perspective of life it is unimaginable that a person would seek to have communion with God while choosing not to love, not to wish a brother or a sister well. We cannot say "Yes" to God as "Our Father" as we ask for his forgiveness and say "No" to others as brothers and sisters as we refuse to forgive them. Our option is to live either in communion, in imitation of the God who is a communion of divine Persons, or to live in alienation, cut off from the communion that God wants to have with us. To opt for alienation is to choose the way of disharmony, to live with inner turmoil and lack of peace.

Refusing forgiveness creates disharmony, fills the heart with resentment and bitterness, and takes away inner peace. Our forgiveness of others brings with it peace of mind because it re-establishes or restores communion. Salvation is the restoration of communion with God to be lived in communion with others. When that communion is lost, disintegration follows. The person loses inner peace because the inner harmony of his or her being, that is communion, has been broken.

**Pastoral sensitivity**

I have learned over the years that in talking to people about forgiveness we have to distinguish between the *broken heart* that feels it cannot forgive a wrong or injustice and the *hardened heart* that is determined not to forgive. The broken heart needs healing; the hardened heart needs conversion. If the person with the broken heart comes to the Lord, seeking healing for his or her inner wounds in Holy Communion, he or she will certainly begin to experience a new peace and joy. As he or she continues to bring his or her hurt to the Lord, that person will receive the grace to forgive and experience inner healing of the hurt. It is only forgiveness that heals the broken heart. There is no other medicine. That is, of course, the reason why Jesus asks us to forgive "not seven, but seventy-seven times" (Matthew 18:22). He said, "I have come so that they may have life and have it to the full" (John 10:10). The "seventy-seven times" forgiveness is the secret of how to have life to the full. We will consider this in more detail in Chapter Seven.

Forgiving from the heart never means condoning or excusing or tolerating unjust behaviour. Nor does forgiving from the heart mean that we must forgo our rights to justice. There is no conflict between forgiving from the heart and seeking justice. Forgiving from the heart means that, while we acknowledge before God the wrong that has been done, we are willing to accept the wrongdoer as a brother or sister whom Jesus has redeemed, just as he has redeemed us. When one's heart is broken, forgiveness may initially seem impossible. But, as the person comes to receive Our Lord in Holy Communion and to be received by the Lord, and asks for the grace to forgive, the broken heart begins to heal and the person comes into full freedom and peace once again.

In the very reception of Holy Communion we remember that we never receive the sacrament as isolated individuals. We always receive Holy Communion in union with all our brothers and sisters. This means that the same Lord who is receiving us, as we come forward to receive Holy Communion, is also receiving or willing to receive those who may have sinned against us. If there is anyone in your life at this time who is causing you a lot of distress, Holy Communion will be a time of great inner healing if, as you receive Our Lord, you ask him to receive and bless that person. Fr Raniero Cantalamessa expresses this well when he writes:

> When we want a more intimate communion with Jesus or we need forgiveness or a special grace from him, this is the way to obtain it: to welcome Jesus in Communion together with that particular brother or sister. We can say clearly: "Jesus, I receive you today together with... (better if we here name the person); I'll keep him or her in my heart with you; I shall be happy if you bring him or her with you". This little act is very pleasing to Jesus because he knows that it causes us to die a little.[6]

In receiving Jesus in Holy Communion we always need to ask him for the grace to receive and welcome every person whom he receives and welcomes. Since he is in them we cannot really

---

6 Raniero Cantalamessa, *The Eucharist* (Collegeville: Liturgical Press, 1995), p. 38.

accept him if we reject them. Holy Communion is for us the time to receive the grace to forgive from the heart.

Those who are determined not to forgive are opting for a life without the grace of God, without communion in the Spirit, without being one within the Body of Christ. They are in great spiritual need. They need conversion. They should really beg the Lord, if they receive Holy Communion, for the grace to do for others what God wants to do for them. God wants to forgive them, but to receive God's forgiveness they must be ready to forgive others. Daily we ask God for forgiveness and daily we need the grace to forgive.

**Behold the Lamb of God**
Just before we come forward to receive Holy Communion, we pray: "Lamb of God, you take away the sins of the world, have mercy on us." And then the priest may pray silently this wonderful prayer:

> Lord Jesus Christ, Son of the living God,
> who, by the will of the Father
> and the work of the Holy Spirit,
> through your Death gave life to the world,
> free me by this, your most holy Body and Blood,
> from all my sins and from every evil;
> keep me always faithful to your commandments,
> and never let me be parted from you.

That prayer is a summary of our whole faith in the redeeming love of Christ. We are praying to be freed from all sin and protected from all evil. I always regret that the priest says this prayer silently because it is a prayer for the whole community and it should be prayed by each of us as we prepare for Holy Communion.

We are now almost ready to receive the Lord in Holy Communion and so the Church, mindful of our sinfulness, reassures us of God's great mercy. The Church has always encouraged us to purify our hearts before we approach Holy Communion. This work of purification is God's work, not ours. God has promised us, "I shall pour clean water over you and you will be cleansed; I shall cleanse you of all your defilement and all your idols. I shall give you a new heart, and put a new spirit in you" (Ezekiel 36:25-26). Jesus wants to fulfil the Father's great promise to us by purifying our hearts as we prepare ourselves for an ever deeper communion with him.

**Sacrament of confession**

The Church encourages us to have a regular practice of celebrating the sacrament of reconciliation as we live our sacramental, Eucharistic life. If we have fallen into serious sin then, of course, we should always "go to confession" before we receive Holy Communion. This is the great sacrament of forgiveness that Christ gave to the Church when he said to the apostles on Easter Sunday evening, "Receive the Holy Spirit. For those whose sins you forgive, they are forgiven" (John 20:22-23). We hear these reassuring words of absolution as the priest prays, "God, the Father of mercies… sent the Holy Spirit among us for the forgiveness of sins… I absolve you from your sins in the name of the Father, and of the Son, and of the Holy Spirit." The forgiveness of our sins is the work of the Holy Spirit. Not only does the Holy Spirit forgive all our sins but the Spirit also heals the wounds that our sins and the sins of others against us have inflicted on us. As the Catechism says:

> Healing the wounds of sin, the Holy Spirit renews us interiorly through a spiritual transformation. He enlightens and strengthens us to live as "children of light" through "all that is good and right and true".[7]

Very often it is the "healing [of] the wounds of sin" that have been inflicted by others, and not just the forgiveness of our own sins,

---

7  *Catechism of the Catholic Church*, 1695.

that is the great blessing of the sacrament of confession. Indeed, Blessed Paul VI, in his introduction to the new *Rite of Penance*, said, "Just as the wound of sin is varied and multiple in the life of individuals and of the community, so the healing which penance provides is varied."[8] There can be a multiple wound inflicted by the sins of others. The very best thing to do when deeply hurt by someone is to go to confession and receive healing for the wound of sin that has been inflicted and then joyfully celebrate the Eucharist and receive Holy Communion.

We began the celebration of the Mass by confessing our sins and asking for God's forgiveness. Now, just before we come forward to receive Holy Communion, the priest holds up the sacred host and proclaims,

> Behold the Lamb of God,
> behold him who takes away the sins of the world.
> Blessed are those called to the supper of the Lamb.

To which we respond,

> Lord, I am not worthy
> that you should enter under my roof,
> but only say the word
> and my soul shall be healed.

In the presence of the Lamb of God all our sins, even the greatest, are forgiven once our hearts are truly sorry for them. We can then approach the altar with humble and grateful confidence knowing that, as we say in Eucharistic Prayer II, the Lord counts us "worthy to be in [his] presence and minister to [him]". We need this reassurance because the devil always tries to undermine our sense of joy and union with Jesus by reminding us of our sinfulness. In the intimate moment of personal communion with Jesus we believe the word of the Lord, "As far as the east is from the west, so far

---

8  Paul VI, *Rite of Penance*, 7.

does he remove our sins" (Psalm 103:12). Good people sometimes cling on to their guilt, despite the assurance of God's forgiveness, and continue to live a joyless life because of their past sins. They need to take to heart the opening words of Pope Francis' great apostolic exhortation:

> The joy of the gospel fills the hearts and lives of all who encounter Jesus. Those who accept his offer of salvation are set free from sin, sorrow, inner emptiness and loneliness.[9]

Jesus tells us that he wants us to have this joy. He says, "I have told you this so that my joy may be in you and your joy be complete" (John 15:11). In the moment of Holy Communion we open our hearts in loving confidence to receive this complete joy from the Lord.

Jesus invites us to receive Holy Communion and to enter into a deep personal and intimate union with him. He says to us,

> Come to me all you who labour and are overburdened and I will give you rest. Shoulder my yoke and learn from me, for I am gentle and humble in heart, and you will find rest for your souls. Yes, my yoke is easy and my burden light (Matthew 11:28-30).

If we are burdened with worries about the family or struggles in the parish, anxieties about our health or about the future, fears arising from addictions of any kind, the Lord is inviting us to bring all to him. We have already offered everything to the Lord as we placed our gifts on the altar. Now we have the great grace in Holy Communion to personally lay down all our burdens and be filled with joyful hope. As St John Paul II wrote, "The Eucharist... plants a seed of living hope in our daily commitment to the work before us."[10] This living hope enables us to reach out beyond all our current troubles and embrace the future that God has in store for us. The future will be God's gift.

---

9 Pope Francis, *Evangelii Gaudium*, 1.
10 John Paul II, *Ecclesia de Eucharistia*, 20.

**Receiving and being received**

As we come forward to receive Holy Communion at Mass we may sometimes forget that, in the words of St John Paul II:

> *Each of us receives Christ,* but also… *Christ receives each of us.*[11]

Christ received us from the moment we entered the sacred assembly to celebrate the Mass. He was there to meet us and welcome us. He invited us to take our place at the table of the word of God and spoke to us as the scriptures were being proclaimed. He invited us to "take and eat". Now, in Holy Communion, Jesus takes us, all of us, including those I may have problems with, into his heart in a very personal and intimate way, making us all one with him. This is the moment when we do what he asked us to do when he said, "Take and eat, this is my body," and "Take and drink, this is my blood." In fact, it was for this moment that Lord came into the world. He said to his apostles and he says to us, "I have longed to eat this passover with you before I suffer" (Luke 22:15). This is the hour when he fulfils the mission the Father gave him when he sent him into the world: "I have come so that they may have life and have it to the full" (John 10:10).

For this fullness of life we need the "bread of life". Jesus says, "It is my Father who gives you the bread from heaven, the true bread; for the bread of God is that which comes down from heaven and gives life to the world" (John 6:32-33). As we come forward to receive Holy Communion it is the Father who gives us "the bread from heaven", Jesus, who is "the bread of life", and it is Jesus himself who receives us into his divine life with the Father. We should take time to ponder deeply this amazing truth that, as we come to the altar to receive Holy Communion, it is God the Father who is giving us the new "manna from heaven", "the bread of life" that is Jesus, the Lamb of God, our paschal sacrifice.

---

11 Ibid., 22.

Jesus says to us, "Make your home in me, as I make mine in you" (John 15:4). Holy Communion is the sacred moment when we abide in Christ and Christ abides in us in such an intimate and personal way that he becomes "the bread of life" that gives us his own divine life. Speaking at his first World Youth Day in Cologne in August 2005, Benedict XVI said to a million young people:

> The Body and Blood of Christ are given to us so that we ourselves will be transformed in our turn. We are to become the Body of Christ, his own Flesh and Blood. We all eat the one bread, and this means that we ourselves become one. In this way, adoration... becomes union. God no longer simply stands before us as the One who is totally Other. He is within us, and we are in him. His dynamic enters into us and then seeks to spread outwards to others until it fills the world, so that his love can truly become the dominant measure of the world.[12]

## We become what we eat

Christ enters our hearts in Holy Communion so to transform us that we become his body in this world. In the words of St Leo the Great, "Our partaking of the Body and Blood of Christ tends only to make us become what we eat."[13] The living bread that we eat in Holy Communion is not transformed into our body, rather we are transformed into Christ's body. St Augustine expressed this amazing truth in this way: "He who suffered for us has entrusted to us in this Sacrament his Body and Blood, which indeed he has even made us. For we have been made his Body, and by his mercy, we are that which we receive."[14] Our Holy Communion, therefore, is much more than receiving Christ into our hearts, wonderful though that is. It is Christ receiving us so completely into his heart that we become one Spirit with him. Each time we receive Holy Communion we become more deeply one with Christ.

---

12 Benedict XVI, Homily, World Youth Day, Cologne, 21 August 2005.
13 St Leo the Great, Sermon 12 on the Passion, as cited in Cantalamessa, *The Eucharist*, p. 39.
14 Cited in James T. O'Connor, *The Hidden Manna: Theology of the Eucharist* (San Francisco: Ignatius Press, 1988), p. 61.

**Sharing Christ's hour**

St John introduces his account of the Last Supper and passion with these words: "It was before the festival of the Passover, and Jesus knew that the hour had come for him to pass from this world to the Father" (John 13:1). Jesus wants us to be with him in his hour. As Benedict XVI said:

> Jesus left us the task of entering into his "hour". The Eucharist draws us into Jesus' act of self-oblation. More than just statically receiving the incarnate *Logos*, we enter into the very dynamic of his self-giving.[15]

Our response to Christ's self-giving love is our own desire to reciprocate with self-giving love by entering into Holy Communion with Christ. And, no matter how half-hearted we may feel we are, once we "enter into the very dynamic of Christ's self-giving" our own self-giving is purified, enlivened and enables us to discover our true selves. As the Second Vatican Council said, people "can fully discover their true selves only in sincere self-giving".[16] In our Holy Communion, Christ shares with us the "dynamic of his self-giving" and activates and strengthens our own self-giving.

**Speaking the language of love**

Our Holy Communion is a time of most intimate love with Jesus who receives us into his heart. We have to speak the language of love, the language of the heart. We should talk, heart to heart, with Jesus about everything that is going on in our lives. That is what intimate friends do. They don't have secrets. Jesus, of course, already knows everything about us and so we can conceal nothing from him. But, if we don't want to talk about it, he will not raise it with us. He will wait until we are ready to share more deeply as we grow in trust. St Alphonsus Liguori, the founder of my Religious Congregation, the Redemptorists, was a passionate lover of Jesus and he poured out his heart to him each time "he entered into his

---

15 Benedict XVI, *Sacramentum Caritatis*, 11.
16 *Gaudium et Spes*, Pastoral Constitution on the Church in the Modern World, 24.

hour" and received Holy Communion. His marvellous book *The Holy Eucharist* is full of great insights and devotion. This exuberant heart-to-heart conversation with Jesus shows us how a true lover speaks to his beloved:

> O my Jesus, this is what I seek of you, and what I will always seek of you in the Holy Communion: "Let us be always united, and never more be separated." I know that you will not separate yourself from me, if I do not first separate myself from you. But this is my fear, lest I should in future separate myself from you by sin, as I have done in times past. O my blessed Redeemer, permit it not: Suffer me not to be separated from you. As long as I am alive, I am in danger of this; oh, through the merits of your death, I beseech you let me die, rather than repeat this great injury against you. I repeat it, and pray you to grant me your grace always to repeat: "Suffer me not to be separated from you, suffer me not to be separated from you". O God of my soul, I love you; I love you, and I will always love you.[17]

That is the passionate language of the lover, afraid he might in the slightest way offend his beloved, and fearing the greatest of all evils, which would be to be separated from his beloved.

## The Holy Trinity and Holy Communion

Our union with Jesus in Holy Communion is so personal and intimate that we may often overlook the deeper mystery of this union. When the apostle Philip said to Jesus, "Lord, let us see the Father and then we shall be satisfied," Jesus said to him, "Have I been with you all this time, Philip... and you still do not know me? To have seen me is to have seen the Father, so how can you say, 'Let us see the Father'? Do you not believe that I am in the Father and the Father is in me?" (John 14:8-10). Jesus also emphasised

---

17 St Alphonsus de Liguori, *The Holy Eucharist*, Centenary Edition, ed. E. Grimm (New York: Benziger, 1887), p. 221.

his unity with the Father when he said, "the Father and I are one" (John 10:30). And in his great prayer for the unity of his disciples Jesus said,

> May they all be one.
> Father, may they be one in us,
> as you are in me and I am in you,
> so that the world may believe it was you who sent me.
> I have given them the glory you gave to me,
> that they may be one as we are one.
> With me in them and you in me,
> may they be so completely one
> that the world will realise that it was you who sent me
> and that I have loved them as much as you loved me
> (John 17:21-23).

This great prayer that Jesus made to God the Father is fulfilled in our Holy Communion. We enter into communion, not only with Jesus but also with the Father, and not just with the Father but with one another. The bond of our unity is the Holy Spirit. As Fr Cantalamessa says:

> In the Eucharist the Holy Spirit gives us Christ in the consecration, and Christ gives us the Holy Spirit in the Communion.[18]

Our Communion in Mass manifests the profound mystery of our Church which is, in the words of the Second Vatican Council:

> A people made one by the unity of the Father, the Son and the Holy Spirit.[19]

Our unity becomes manifest in the congregation as we all move as one body to receive the Body and Blood of Jesus. We are not approaching the altar as isolated individuals. We are coming

---

18 Cantalamessa, *The Eucharist*, p. 30.
19 *Lumen Gentium*, Dogmatic Constitution on the Church, 4.

as "a people made one", as the body of Christ. Our intimate, personal relationship with Jesus in Holy Communion is never an individualistic relationship. It cannot be reduced to "me and my Jesus". It is always a communal relationship, a trinitarian relationship, while being at the same time deeply personal and intimate.

## Our thanksgiving after Communion

In our thanksgiving we should acknowledge that it is from the Father and through the Holy Spirit that we have received the gift of Jesus in Holy Communion. If, as Jesus said to Philip, "to have seen me is to have seen the Father", then surely it is also true that to receive Jesus is to receive the Father. It is good and at times, perhaps, necessary to remind ourselves that each of us equally receives Jesus and with him the Father and the Holy Spirit in Holy Communion. No one receives more than anyone else. Your worst enemy receives the same Lord as you and your best friend. Our traditional practice of taking some time after Communion in personal thanksgiving is an opportunity to have a more intimate conversation with the Lord. Jesus has entered our heart and our thanksgiving enables us to spend some time alone with him. This is the time when we can talk to Our Lord about everything in our life while at the same time thanking him for all his love and forgiveness. The more we thank him, the more he fills our hearts with gratitude to the Father. This gratitude is the great "Eucharistic gift" because the very name of our sacrament, the Eucharist, means "gratitude". The more we allow the Lord to fill our hearts with gratitude, during our thanksgiving, the more we will be freed from all negativity about others, about life and indeed about ourselves.

## The manifestation of the Church

Alexander Schmemann expresses the truth we have been pondering in this way:

The Eucharist is not "one of the sacraments" or one of the services, but the very manifestation and fulfilment of the Church in all her power, sanctity and fullness.[20]

The Eucharist is the "manifestation and fulfilment of the Church" because in the Eucharist we become what Christ desires: we become one with Christ; through Christ we become one with God the Father; by our union with Christ and the Father through the gift of the Holy Spirit we become the body of Christ on earth. As Benedict XVI said,

> In the most blessed Eucharist is contained the entire spiritual wealth of the Church, namely Christ himself our Pasch and our living bread, who gives life to humanity through his flesh – that flesh which is given life and gives life by the Holy Spirit.[21]

In our Holy Communion, therefore, Jesus wants so to fill us with his Holy Spirit that our lives will be transformed into him. He yearns to give us all the grace and all the gifts of the Spirit that we need to live our lives as his faithful disciples. St Paul says,

> Now this Lord is the Spirit, and where the Spirit of the Lord is, there is freedom. And we, with our unveiled faces reflecting like mirrors the brightness of the Lord, all grow brighter and brighter as we are turned into the image that we reflect; this is the work of the Lord who is Spirit (2 Corinthians 3:17-18).

In our Holy Communion this transformation is happening. We do not see it ourselves because we always remain conscious of being sinners. No saint ever saw himself or herself as holy or sinless. Saints echo what St Paul wrote to Timothy: "Christ Jesus came into the world to save sinners. I myself am the greatest of them" (1 Timothy 1:15). St Paul rejoiced in being "the greatest" sinner

---

20 Alexander Schmemann, *The Eucharist: Sacrament of the Kingdom* (New York: St Vladimir's Seminary Press, 2000), p. 25.
21 Benedict XVI, *Sacramentum Caritatis*, 16.

because he believed with total conviction that Jesus Christ saved him from his sins. And, we should remember, it is only through the light of the Holy Spirit that we can become aware of our sins. When we approach Holy Communion with a sincere and contrite heart we believe that all our sins are forgiven and the miracle of our transformation in Christ is taking place. We become what we receive; we become the body of Christ.

**I will raise them up on the last day**

Jesus said to the people in the synagogue at Capernaum:

> I tell you most solemnly,
> if you do not eat the flesh of the Son of Man
> and drink his blood,
> you will not have life in you.
> Anyone who does eat my flesh and drink my blood
> has eternal life,
> and I shall raise him up on the last day (John 6:53-54).

In our Holy Communion we do what Jesus asks us to do. We eat the "bread of life" and we drink from "the chalice of salvation". St Ignatius of Antioch, one of the early Fathers of the Church, who was martyred around AD 108, called the Eucharist:

> The medicine of immortality, the antidote for death, and the food that makes us live for ever in Jesus Christ.[22]

Ignatius himself, when he wrote those words to the Church in Ephesus, was on his way to his martyrdom in Rome. But for him, as a man of faith, death in this world opened the door to the eternal life that Jesus had for him. When we receive Holy Communion Jesus wants to assure us that he has that same eternal life for us. He will raise us up on the last day. Because of original sin we all have to pass through the valley of death but, on the other side of the

---

22 Cited in *Catechism of the Catholic Church*, 1405.

grave, we reach the shores of eternity. The Eucharist is the pledge of our eternal glory. The Catechism teaches:

> In an ancient prayer the Church acclaims the mystery of the Eucharist: "O sacred banquet in which Christ is received as food, the memory of his Passion is renewed, the soul is filled with grace and a pledge of the life to come is given to us."[23]

When we receive Our Lord in Holy Communion we should always thank him that he is guaranteeing our eternal life, that he will fulfil his promise and raise us up on the last day and that we, with all our family and loved ones, will live for ever with him in glory. In every Mass we remember all those who have died: "Remember also those who have died in the peace of your Christ and all the dead, whose faith you alone have known."[24] And in every Mass, as we saw in the last chapter, we say several times to Our Lord that we are looking forward to his return in glory. Because the Eucharist is "the medicine of immortality" we can be joyful when we think about dying and what happens after we die. As we receive Holy Communion we should try to open our hearts to the full grace that Jesus has come to give us. Here and now he is receiving us into an intimate communion with himself, filling us with the Holy Spirit, and enabling us to rejoice in faith, believing that we will live for ever with his Father and with his mother Mary and with all the saints in heaven. Jesus is truly the "life-giving bread" that has come down from heaven. What could we do without Holy Communion? As St John Paul II said:

> In the Eucharist we have Jesus, we have his redemptive sacrifice, we have his resurrection, we have the gift of the Holy Spirit, we have adoration, obedience and love of the Father. Were we to disregard the Eucharist, how could we overcome our own deficiency?[25]

---

23 *Catechism of the Catholic Church*, 1402.
24 Eucharistic Prayer IV.
25 John Paul II, *Ecclesia de Eucharistia*, 60.

God the Father, in his great redeeming love, sacramentally renewed and made present to us in Mass, gives us Jesus his Son as the "bread of life" and, as we receive Jesus in Holy Communion, he fills us with the Holy Spirit. Holy Communion is for us our sanctification, because, as we eat the "bread of life", we become what we eat. We become the body of Christ. We become the Eucharist we celebrate.

# Chapter Six

# Attuning our minds to our voices

During Mass we say some wonderful prayers to God, prayers that express the truth about God and the truth about ourselves. But before these prayers can form in us a habitual way of seeing ourselves in the light of these truths, we have to conform our minds to the words we are saying. We have to mean what we are saying. The Second Vatican Council expressed it this way:

> In order that the liturgy may be able to produce its full effects it is necessary that the faithful come to it with proper dispositions, that their minds be attuned to their voices, and that they cooperate with heavenly grace lest they receive it in vain.[1]

In this chapter we want to take a closer look at what we are actually saying to God in our prayers during Mass. Our assumption is that we mean what we say when we speak to God. But our experience can also reveal that, far from meaning what we say, we are often resisting the truth expressed in the prayers.

## The truth about God

When we gather for the Mass we constitute "the sacred assembly" of God's people. We do not gather, therefore, as a group of individuals without any real spiritual bond, nor do we gather as a community closed in on itself, concerned only with our own members. We assemble as sons and daughters of God, God's people, open to embrace the whole world as we pray for "all your children scattered throughout the world".[2] The Mass forces us to look beyond ourselves and our own needs. Our conscious participation in the celebration of the Mass challenges us to see

---

1 *Sacrosanctum Concilium*, Constitution on the Sacred Liturgy, 11.
2 Eucharistic Prayer III.

others as God sees them and to be open to others as Christ is open to us. Speaking about how the Eucharist influences the way we think, St Irenaeus could write, "Our way of thinking accords with the Eucharist, and the Eucharist, in turn, confirms our way of thinking."[3] As we consciously say the prayers of the Mass we are proclaiming the truth that God is our loving Father and also that we are all children of God, brothers and sisters of Jesus. We are accepting afresh our relationship with the whole human family as brothers and sisters.

At the very beginning of Mass we are invited by the priest to acknowledge that, like every other brother or sister, we are sinners in need of God's mercy. The priest says, "Brothers and sisters, let us acknowledge our sins, and so prepare ourselves to celebrate the sacred mysteries." We don't come to Mass feeling that we are better than anybody else. We come with the awareness that like everyone else we stand in need of God's mercy and forgiveness. When Pope Francis was asked who he really was, he responded, "I am a sinner whom the Lord has looked upon."[4] That accurately describes each of us. We begin our celebration of Mass in the awareness that each of us is a sinner whom the Lord has looked upon.

When we stand in God's presence acknowledging our need for God's mercy and forgiveness, we are proclaiming the wonderful truth that God is "compassion and love" (Psalm 103:8), our loving Father, who always takes away all our sins as we repent in his presence. We do not make excuses for our sins. Rather, we take full responsibility as we say: "I have greatly sinned, in my thoughts and in my words, in what I have done and in what I have failed to do, through my fault, through my fault, through my most grievous fault." As we take full responsibility for our sins, both as individuals and as a community, God, as it were, takes full responsibility for God's great mercy and compassion and, in the

---

3  Cited in Margaret Scott, *The Eucharist and Social Justice* (New York: Paulist Press, 2008), p. 44.
4  Interview with Fr Antonio Spadaro, September 2013.

words of the psalm, "as far as the east is from the west, so far does he remove our sins" (Psalm 103:12). It is important that we attune our minds to this liberating truth and let go of all guilt or shame. Imagine what a difference it would make to our peace of heart if, at every Mass, we really believed in what we were saying when we asked God for forgiveness! We are proclaiming the truth about God. God is our loving Father who delights in forgiving us, freeing us from our sins, filling us with the grace of the Holy Spirit and making us one with Christ. How consciously do we attune our minds to this wonderful truth? Sometimes people are convinced that God can never forgive them because their sins are so great. One man made a week's retreat with me. He never missed Mass but would not receive Holy Communion. He could not accept that God could forgive him. When he began to see the hidden pride that was actually making him believe that his sin was too big even for God, he was able confess his pride and receive Communion again. Unconsciously he was denying the words of Jesus, that his blood "will be poured out for you and for many for the forgiveness of sins". The love of Jesus, "the Lamb of God... who takes away the sins of the world", could take away his sins too. As he attuned his mind and heart to the words he was praying, he experienced liberation.

**Truth about ourselves**

Our prayers during Mass also proclaim the truth about ourselves. We acknowledge ourselves, not just as sinners, but as redeemed sinners, because in the Mass we are participating in the sacrifice of our redemption. We hear that Christ's blood "will be poured out for you and for many for the forgiveness of sins". We hear these words and we rejoice because we know and accept our need for redemption. St Paul had a vivid awareness of being a sinner in need of redemption, He wrote to his great helper Timothy,

> Here is a saying that you can rely on and nobody should doubt: that Christ Jesus came into the world to save sinners.

I myself am the greatest of them; and if mercy has been shown to me, it is because Jesus Christ meant to make me the greatest evidence of his inexhaustible patience for all the other people who would later have to trust in him to come to eternal life (1 Timothy 1:15-16).

The prayers we say together during Mass constantly remind us of our true identity. We are greeted as "brothers and sisters"; we call God "Our Father"; we listen gratefully to the Father as he speaks to us in the proclamation of the scriptures and we shout out our thanks as we say, "Thanks be to God"; together we offer our gifts of bread and wine to the Father and pray, "Blessed are you, Lord God of all creation, for through your goodness we have received the bread we offer you…"; as the priest adds water to the wine he prays in our name, "By the mystery of this water and wine may we come to share in the divinity of Christ, who humbled himself to share in our humanity." What an extraordinary request we are making in this prayer! We are asking to be divinised. Notice how we have moved from acknowledging that we are sinners in need of God's mercy to asking confidently that we share in the very divinity of Christ. Now we are beginning to see the truth about ourselves. We are sons and daughters of God, brothers and sisters of Christ, destined by God to share fully in the divinity of Christ.

When the priest begins the great prayer of the Preface he invites the congregation to "Lift up your hearts," to which we respond, "We lift them up to the Lord." We should ponder well what we are saying about ourselves. We are saying to each other that we have lifted our hearts up to the Lord. The whole congregation is now united in the same great act of worship in lifting up their hearts to God. That is how the Mass teaches us to see each other. We are people with "uplifted hearts", people who know God as our loving Father, who know Jesus as our saviour and brother, who know the

Holy Spirit as our sanctifier and unifier, who know one another as brothers and sisters in the Lord. We conclude the great prayer of the Preface of each Mass by uniting our voices with the voices of the angels as we pray in words such as these,

> And so, with Angels and Archangels,
> with Thrones and Dominions,
> and with all the hosts and Powers of heaven,
> we sing the hymn of your glory,
> as without end we acclaim:

> Holy, Holy, Holy Lord God of hosts.
> Heaven and earth are full of your glory.
> Hosanna in the highest.
> Blessed is he who comes in the name of the Lord.
> Hosanna in the highest.[5]

This wonderful acclamation reveals how in faith we see our world. If we look at the world without the vision of faith we will not see it full of the glory of God. We will see injustice and divisions, famines and wars, and all the consequences of human sinfulness. We will see only "the fallen world". But with our "uplifted hearts" we can see the world for which Christ our Lord gave his life on the cross, the world that has been redeemed through the blood of Christ. And, despite everything that is wrong in the world, we are emboldened to proclaim that the deeper reality is that God's world is "full of your glory". This is not an escape from the cruel realities that we see around us. On the contrary, it provides us with the energy and the confidence to confront the injustice that plagues the world.

### Eucharistic amazement

With our uplifted hearts, in union with "all the hosts of heaven", we now continue the great Eucharistic Prayer. When it comes to the moment of the consecration, all the attention of our mind and heart is focused on the altar as the priest imposes his hands over our

---

5 Preface I of the Sundays in Ordinary Time.

gifts of bread and wine and begins the great invocation of the Holy Spirit. He appeals to God the Father:

> Make holy, therefore, these gifts, we pray,
> by sending down your Spirit upon them like the dewfall,
> so that they may become for us
> the Body and Blood of our Lord Jesus Christ.[6]

God does that. Now in faith we behold on the altar the very Body and Blood of our Saviour Jesus Christ and we are filled with what St John Paul II called "Eucharistic 'amazement'". He wrote, "I would like to rekindle this Eucharistic 'amazement' by the present Encyclical Letter."[7] We are now at the very heart of the mystery of our salvation, the mystery of the Father's abiding love for us. Amazement, awe, reverence, gratitude, joy – these are just some of the sentiments that the mystery of the Mass kindles in our hearts. We have to attune our minds and open our hearts to what we are saying and to what we are believing at this moment of the Mass.

In response to the priest's proclamation: "The mystery of faith", the second of the acclamations given in the Missal is:

> When we eat this Bread and drink this Cup,
> we proclaim your Death, O Lord,
> until you come again.

We place ourselves in a very personal relationship with Jesus when we say, "we proclaim your Death, O Lord". We are speaking directly to Jesus on the altar, under the appearance of the bread and wine that we brought to the altar. Jesus wants us to have a heart-to-heart relationship with him. Indeed, he wants to be welcomed in our hearts when we receive him in Holy Communion. Without this heart-to-heart relationship, this personal encounter with Christ, our celebration of the Mass may remain ritualistic or even legalistic. One woman said to me after I had given a talk on the Eucharist, "I need a big grace. I just go to Mass because I don't want to commit

---

6 Eucharistic Prayer II.
7 John Paul II, *Ecclesia de Eucharistia*, 6.

a sin by not going. Now I want to go to Mass because I want to be in communion with Jesus and with everyone else. I want to make that gift of myself to God at the offertory and receive back from the altar the gift of the risen and glorified Christ so that I can truly be one with Christ and with all my brothers and sisters." She had begun to attune her mind and heart to the words that she had been saying at Mass for years. She understood clearly what Pope Francis meant when he said:

> The Eucharist is the sacrament of communion that brings us out of individualism so that we may follow him together, living out our faith in him. Therefore we should all ask ourselves before the Lord: how do I live the Eucharist? Do I live it anonymously or as a moment of true communion with the Lord, and also with all the brothers and sisters who share this same banquet?[8]

**One body, one spirit in Christ**

The great invocation of the Holy Spirit in the Mass does not end at the consecration. After the priest invokes the Holy Spirit to come upon our gifts he invokes the Spirit to come upon all of us to make us one in Christ. Let us look at some of these wonderful prayers:

> Humbly we pray
> that, partaking of the Body and Blood of Christ,
> we may be gathered into one by the Holy Spirit.[9]

> Grant that we, who are nourished
> by the Body and Blood of your Son
> and filled with his Holy Spirit,
> may become one body, one spirit, in Christ.[10]

> Look, O Lord, upon the Sacrifice
> which you yourself have provided for your Church,
> and grant in your loving kindness

---

8   Pope Francis, Homily on the Solemnity of Corpus Christi, Thursday 30 May 2013.
9   Eucharistic Prayer II.
10 Eucharistic Prayer III.

> to all who partake of this one Bread and one Chalice
> that, gathered into one body by the Holy Spirit,
> they may truly become a living sacrifice in Christ
> to the praise of your glory.[11]

In these inspiring prayers we are asking God the Father so to unite us with Christ, through the Holy Spirit, that we will be "one body, one spirit in Christ". We are praying that the Holy Spirit will heal all our divisions and restore us to full communion with one another. We are asking to become "a living sacrifice in Christ". We must try to attune our minds to these words and open our hearts to receive this transforming grace from God. Do we really want God to answer this prayer for unity? We prayed during the offertory "to share in the divinity of Christ". Jesus wants to bless us with this transforming grace of divinisation. Are we ready and willing to receive this transformation? How will it impact on my life? What will it do to my relationships with others? Jesus says to us, "He who eats my flesh and drinks my blood lives in me and I live in him" (John 6:56). What does it mean for us to live in Christ and for Christ to live in us? Great saints and mystics down through the ages have tried to put into words this unique relationship that we have with Jesus. St John Eudes tried to explain this profound mystery of our union with Christ with these words:

> Remember that our Lord Jesus Christ is your true head and that you are one of his members. He is to you as the head is to the members of the body; all that is his is yours. His spirit, his heart, his body, his soul, all his faculties, all are to be used by you as if they were your own, so that serving him you may praise him, love him, glorify him. For your part, you are to him as a member to the head, and he earnestly desires to use all your faculties as if they were his own for the service and glorification of his Father.[12]

---

11 Eucharistic Prayer IV.
12 *The Divine Office*, vol. III, Office of Readings, Feast of St John Eudes, 19 August.

Just as the bread and wine become the Body and Blood of Christ by the power of the Holy Spirit so, through the same Holy Spirit, we become Christ's body in this world. As St Paul said so emphatically, "you together are Christ's body" (1 Corinthians 12:27). Christ is the head and we are the members of his body. In the members of your family you meet Christ and they meet Christ in you. In all your relationships, Christ is present and he speaks and acts through you. This is the grace we ask for when we pray that through the Holy Spirit we will become "one body, one spirit in Christ".

**True self-esteem**

Having prayed that the Holy Spirit may make us "one body, one spirit in Christ", we then make another extraordinary request. We pray,

> May he make of us
> an eternal offering to you,
> so that we may obtain an inheritance with your elect.[13]

This is a breathtaking request. Notice how we see ourselves in this prayer. We see ourselves as people who can be an eternal gift to God the Father. In the words of consecration we heard Christ's words: "my Blood… will be poured out for you and for many for the forgiveness of sins". We believe that through the Blood of Christ, shed for us, all our sins are forgiven. We have been washed clean and now we see ourselves through the redeeming eyes of Jesus who presents us to his Father as an eternal gift. In this prayer we no longer see ourselves through the distorted vision of our own sinfulness but through the victorious eyes of Jesus, who has redeemed us and united us to himself and now presents us to his Father. This is the great redeeming grace and gift of the Mass. In the secret of our hearts, where we know our need for redemption, we can now believe that Christ has brought us into the very presence of his Father. Christ is saying to the Father, "When

---

13 Eucharistic Prayer III.

you see them you see me, because I have become one with them and they have become one with me." It takes time to ponder this profound mystery. St Paul said, "And for anyone who is in Christ, there is a new creation: the old order has gone and a new being is there to see. It is all God's work" (2 Corinthians 5:17-18).

We began the Eucharistic Prayer with the great prayer of the Preface proclaiming that we were joining our voices with the angels and the archangels and the whole host of heaven. Now, having asked that Christ may make us an eternal gift to the Father who is in heaven, we begin to remember the saints in heaven. We pray that

> we may obtain an inheritance with your elect,
> especially with the most Blessed Virgin Mary, Mother of
> God,
> with blessed Joseph, her Spouse,
> with your blessed Apostles and glorious Martyrs
> and with all the Saints.[14]

We consciously take our place with them in God's family. They are no longer distant from us. They are joining us in our worship of God. We remind God the Father that we rely on their "constant intercession in your presence… for unfailing help". When we are making our way to join the Eucharistic community for Mass it is very helpful to remind ourselves that we will be joining not only those whom we see in the church but also the whole communion of saints in heaven. They are already praying for us and awaiting our arrival to join with them in the great act of worship that is the Mass. The members of our own family who have died and are now with God will be joining us for Mass.

**Our reconciliation**

United as one in Christ through the Holy Spirit, we pray for the whole human race:

---

14 Eucharistic Prayer III.

> May this Sacrifice of our reconciliation,
> we pray, O Lord,
> advance the peace and salvation of all the world.[15]

Those are the great gifts that Christ brings to our troubled world from the Father. We ask for this gift of peace with confidence. There may be a situation in our own lives badly in need of peace and salvation at this time. We have already offered that situation to God as our gifts of bread and wine were being brought to the altar. Those gifts represented "all that is within us" (Psalm 103:1), everything about us. Attuning our minds now to this great prayer we open our hearts to receive the gift of peace for ourselves and for everyone in our lives. Notice that we are asking for the gift of peace through "this Sacrifice of our reconciliation". We have been reconciled with God, we have become "an eternal offering" to God and now we can stand in God's presence and ask our Father for his gifts. He will not refuse. We pray in the first place for our Pope and bishop, for the clergy and all God's faithful people. We next appeal to the merciful Father to "gather to yourself all your children scattered throughout the world".[16] This is a most inclusive prayer, a truly Catholic prayer. Nobody is excluded from our prayer in Mass because now we are the body of Christ and Christ died for all. We pray not just for the living but also for those who have died. We pray for "our brothers and sisters who have fallen asleep in the hope of the resurrection"[17] and we pray for "all the dead, whose faith you alone have known".[18] This is an all-embracing prayer for all the dead because God alone knows who welcomed the gift of faith that God offers to each person.

There is, therefore, no person or group of people for whom we do not pray during the Mass. Nor is there any situation in the world for which we do not request "peace and salvation". During the bidding prayers at Mass, people make very specific prayers of intercession

---

15 Ibid.
16 Ibid.
17 Eucharistic Prayer II.
18 Eucharistic Prayer IV.

for those who are sick, for people who are living through war or some natural disaster, for their families and for their parish. The prayers of the Mass are for the whole world and every person on planet Earth. Just as there is nobody excluded from the prayers of the Church during Mass, so there should be nobody excluded from our prayers as we join in those prayers of the Mass. When helping people who find themselves in conflict and strife with someone, I always ask them, "How do you pray for this person?" Too often I get the response, "I never do." They have been joining in those wonderful prayers of the Mass for everyone and every situation but not really attuning their minds to what they were saying. They were excluding or ignoring someone or some group in God's presence.

**The great Amen**
At the conclusion of the great Eucharistic Prayer the priest lifts up the chalice and the consecrated host and proclaims:

> Through him, and with him, and in him,
> O God, almighty Father,
> in the unity of the Holy Spirit,
> all glory and honour is yours,
> for ever and ever.

We all respond with a loud "Amen". That little word "Amen" expresses our full agreement with the whole prayer of the Mass. It means, "Yes, we agree; yes, it is true." It is true that it is only through Christ and with Christ and in Christ that we can give glory to God the Father. In this great proclamation we are acknowledging that we are now in Christ, that we stand in the Father's presence with Christ. In fact, we are proclaiming that when the Father sees us, he sees Christ, because we have become one with Christ his Son. In this prayer we do not give in to any misgivings about our worthiness to be in God's presence. After the consecration, we give God "thanks that you have held us worthy to be in your presence and minister to you".[19] We never stand alone before God. We are always in Christ. We have asked the Father to make us one with Christ through the Holy Spirit and now we are rejoicing that the Father has answered our prayer. So we can say our "Amen". At the beginning of the Preface of the Mass we were asked to "Lift up your hearts", to which we responded, "We lift them up to the Lord." Now, at the conclusion of the Eucharistic Prayer, we respond to this great proclamation of giving all glory to God through Christ with our "uplifted hearts" and we shout out our "Amen". We should always try to put our "uplifted hearts" into the great Amen. As the liturgical scholar A.G. Mortimort wrote:

> If the amen is the most important of the acclamations and replies of biblical origin then, that which concludes the Canon, is the most important in the whole liturgy; much must be made of it.[20]

**The Lord's Prayer**

All the prayers of the Mass have prepared our minds and hearts to join in the great prayer that Jesus gave us. The priest introduces this prayer with these words: "At the Saviour's command and formed by divine teaching, we dare to say". We say together: "Our Father..." We needed that divine teaching to truly believe that God is our loving Father. We can now come to him with great confidence. We come to him, not as isolated individuals, but as his family, as the brothers and sisters of Jesus. We say, "Our Father", not "my Father". We need Christ's redemption before we can truly speak the word "our". In God's presence, who am I including in that little word "our"? Or am I excluding anyone from being numbered in that word "our"? Benedict XVI wrote:

> When we say the word *our*, we say Yes to the living Church in which the Lord wanted to gather his new family. In this sense the Our Father is at once fully personal and a

---

19 Eucharistic Prayer II.
20 A.G. Mortimort, *The Eucharist* (Dublin: Irish University Press, 1973), p. 170.

thoroughly ecclesial prayer. In praying the Our Father, we pray totally with our own heart, but at the same time we pray in communion with the whole family of God, with the living and the dead, with people of all conditions, cultures, and races. The Our Father overcomes all boundaries and makes us one family.[21]

Really attuning our minds to the words of the Our Father can be a great challenge, especially if we find ourselves in the middle of conflict with people we have loved but from whom we have become estranged. The psalmist complained to God when he found himself in this kind of situation: "All who hate me whisper to each other about me, reckoning I deserve the misery I suffer... Even my closest and most trusted friend, who shared my table, rebels against me" (Psalm 41:7-9). In the Mass we stand before God with every brother and sister, no matter what they may have done or are doing to us right now. We can complain to God about their behaviour. But, of course, we would have already offered all the pain of that bad behaviour to God when we offered our gifts of bread and wine. If we refused to offer the conflict and the hurt and pain of the conflict to God at the offertory, then we should not be too surprised if we find it difficult to include the "enemies" in the "our" with which we address the Father.[22] Before Jesus gave us the Our Father as our great Christian family prayer, he said to us,

> I say this to you: love your enemies and pray for those who persecute you; in this way you will be sons of your Father in heaven, for he causes his sun to rise on bad men as well as good, and his rain to fall on honest and dishonest men alike. For if you love those who love you, what right have you to claim any credit? Even the tax collectors do as much, do they not?... You must therefore be perfect just as your heavenly Father is perfect (Matthew 5:44-48).

---

21 Benedict XVI, *Jesus of Nazareth* (London: Bloomsbury, 2007), p. 141.
22 We will return to reflect on forgiveness in Chapter Seven when we consider the healing power of forgiving from the heart.

We can love our enemies with that love of the Father because, as St Paul says, "the love of God has been poured into our hearts by the Holy Spirit which has been given us" (Romans 5:5).

Jesus teaches us in his great prayer to say to the Father, "hallowed be thy name," to pray for God's kingdom to come and for God's will to be done. Then he teaches us to ask God our Father to forgive us our sins against him in the same way in which we forgive those who sin against us. If we are holding unforgiveness in our heart against anybody we will not be able to really give our consent to this prayer until we move towards forgiveness. To become aware of unforgiveness in our heart, while saying the Lord's Prayer, is the enlightenment of the Holy Spirit. It may make us feel uncomfortable or guilty, but it is drawing our attention to what we have to do to escape from being imprisoned in somebody's sin against us. Each time we come to Mass we should bring the ones we have to forgive with us and sincerely pray for the liberating grace of forgiving from the heart.

**The sign of peace**
After the Lord's Prayer the priest says the great prayer for peace, reminding us that it is Christ's peace that he is talking about:

> Lord Jesus Christ,
> who said to your Apostles:
> Peace I leave you, my peace I give you…

Jesus is offering us his peace, a peace that we can only receive if we are willing to share it. The priest or deacon invites us to share with one another a sign of peace. This is a moment of grace and forgiveness. It can also be the moment when we receive a deep inner healing by offering the sign of peace, not just to the person who is physically close to us in our seats, but to the person who is emotionally close to us, even though at the moment he or she may be hundreds of miles away. I saw this healing happen to a very good Religious Sister. The big block in her spiritual growth was the awareness that she had been born out of wedlock. She never knew who her father was. But when she began to explore why she was feeling so blocked on the path to spiritual renewal, it began to dawn on her that deep in her heart she was full of resentment towards her father. She didn't know whether he was alive or dead, but whenever she tried to get in touch with her emotions about him, it was resentment that surfaced.

As a Religious Sister she had been celebrating Mass with her community every day. She was happily sharing the sign of peace with each Sister. When I said to her that the person she should be sharing the sign of peace with was her father, she looked shocked. Then she said, "I will do it." During the following month she consciously extended her hand in love and forgiveness, at the sign of peace, to her father, wherever he may have been. At the end of the month she was able to share with me the marvellous spiritual graces and deep inner healing that she had received. She understood why she had felt so blocked. It was the stone of resentment in her heart. Now that she had let go of all that deep resentment against the father she never knew, she not only received deep healing in her relationship with her father but she also received true love for him. In fact, she was able, for the first time, to live the fourth commandment, which says, "Honour your father and your mother."

**True spiritual formation**

By attuning our minds to the prayers of the Mass we form within ourselves the attitudes of Christ. This is true Christian formation. St Paul can say very confidently that "we are those who have the mind of Christ" (1 Corinthians 2:16). And writing to the Philippians, he says, "In your minds you must be the same as Christ Jesus: His state was divine, yet he did not cling to his equality with God but emptied himself to assume the condition of a slave, and became as men are" (Philippians 2:5-7). Our prayers at Mass challenge us to empty ourselves of every attitude that is unworthy of Christ: prejudice of any kind; indifference towards those in need or suffering from sinful discrimination; harbouring ill feeling or lack of forgiveness towards anyone. In the Mass we stand as the body of Christ before God. We are invited by the prayers we say to allow the Holy Spirit to purify our minds and hearts, by removing from them negativity or bitterness of any kind. We come to Mass, not because we are perfect, but because we need the gift of the Holy Spirit in order to love and forgive, in order to become the Eucharist we celebrate.

We should bring every person, friend or foe, and every situation, pleasant or unpleasant, to the Mass, offer them all to God as we offer ourselves, and then attune our minds and hearts to the prayers of the Mass for each person and each situation. That is how "the mind of Christ" is formed in us and how we begin to love one another as Christ has loved us. As St Irenaeus said:

> Our way of thinking accords with the Eucharist, and the Eucharist, in turn, confirms our way of thinking.[23]

---

23 Cited in Scott, *The Eucharist and Social Justice*, p. 44.

# Chapter Seven

# The healing power of the Eucharist

We know, with the instinct of faith, that the Mass is the supreme act of worship in our lives. In the Mass, perfect worship is offered to God our Father, because in the Mass it is Jesus Christ, our high priest, who is offering us, in union with himself, to the Father. St John Paul II said:

> The Church draws her life from the Eucharist. This truth does not simply express a daily experience of faith, but recapitulates *the heart of the mystery of the Church*. In a variety of ways she joyfully experiences the constant fulfilment of the promise: "Lo, I am with you always, to the close of the age" (Matthew 28:20), but in the Holy Eucharist, through the changing of bread and wine into the body and blood of the Lord, she rejoices in this presence with unique intensity. Ever since Pentecost, when the Church, the People of the New Covenant, began her pilgrim journey towards her heavenly homeland, the Divine Sacrament has continued to mark the passing of her days, filling them with confident hope.[1]

Just as the Church "draws life from the Eucharist", so, too, each of us draws life from the Eucharist. In the Eucharist we have the entire spiritual wealth of the Church. We hear Christ's great promise, "Anyone who does eat my flesh and drink my blood has eternal life, and I shall raise that person up on the last day" (John 6:54). Christ guarantees our eternal life and salvation when we faithfully celebrate the Eucharist. We believe that the Mass is the eternal sacrifice of Christ made present to us sacramentally under the appearance of bread and wine and that as we share in it "the

---

1  John Paul II, *Ecclesia de Eucharistia*, 1.

work of our redemption is accomplished". Consider, for instance, how the Church prays over our gifts of bread and wine that the priest places on the altar:

> Grant us, O Lord, we pray,
> that we may participate worthily in these mysteries,
> for whenever the memorial of this sacrifice is celebrated
> the work of our redemption is accomplished.[2]

Our redemption is being accomplished in the very act of sharing in the Eucharist. Christ's sacrifice, offered once and for all, remains for ever in the presence of God the Father. It is not something that happened two thousand years ago. But how can that sacrifice become present to us? St John Paul II said, "This sacrifice is so decisive for the salvation of the human race that Jesus Christ offered it and returned to the Father only *after he had left us a means of sharing in it* as if we had been present there."[3] This is the amazing gift that Jesus gives us in the Eucharist. His sacrifice for our redemption becomes sacramentally present on the altar as we do as he told us to do, namely, as we take the bread and wine and say, "This is my Body... given up for you," and "This is the chalice of my Blood... poured out for you." We are united with Christ's sacrifice in a unique sacramental way.

Jesus spoke of this redemption in terms of fullness of life. He said, "I have come that they may have life and have it to the full" (John 10:10). This fullness of life is for body, soul and spirit, the health and healing of the whole person. Many of the prayers of the Mass are a direct plea to God for this blessing of health. In this chapter we want to examine some of these prayers so as to deepen our awareness of what the Church is really praying for in her great act of worship in the Mass.[4]

---

2  Prayer over the Offerings, Second Sunday in Ordinary Time.
3  John Paul II, *Ecclesia de Eucharistia*, 11.
4  For further study of the healing ministry see J. McManus C.Ss.R., *The Healing Power of the Sacraments* and *Healing in the Spirit*, both published by Redemptorist Publications.

## Seek first the kingdom of God

We all have many needs in our lives, but the Mass teaches us to get our priorities right. Jesus said, "Set your hearts on his kingdom first, and on his righteousness, and all these other things will be given you as well" (Matthew 6:33). In God's presence, the Mass teaches us to acknowledge first of all our need for God's kingdom, for God's forgiveness and mercy. Our prayer for forgiveness is linked with healing. In our Penitential Act at Mass we may say, "You were sent to heal the contrite of heart: Lord, have mercy." If I am looking for a healing from the Lord I should, first of all, look at the spiritual state of my heart and ask myself, "Do I have a truly contrite heart?" An elderly Presbyterian woman gave me a wonderful example of how to prepare for healing prayer. As she asked me to pray with her, she knelt down and said, "Before you pray, I must ask God to cleanse my heart from all my sins," and she offered a most beautiful prayer, confessing her sins and asking God's forgiveness. Then she said to me, "You can pray now." She understood well what it means when we say, "You were sent to heal the contrite of heart." I must always ask myself, "Am I genuinely sorry for all my sins, the small ones as well as the big ones?" We need the light of faith to recognise sin. The Catechism reminds us:

> Only the light of divine Revelation clarifies the reality of sin and particularly of the sin committed at mankind's origins. Without the knowledge Revelation gives of God we cannot recognise sin clearly and are tempted to explain it as merely a developmental flaw, a psychological weakness, a mistake, or the necessary consequences of an inadequate social structure, etc. Only in the knowledge of God's plan for man can we grasp that sin is an abuse of the freedom that God gives to created persons so that they are capable of loving him and loving one another.[5]

---

5  *Catechism of the Catholic Church*, 387.

In faith we know that sin, because it can separate us from God, is the greatest of all evils. That is why, at the beginning of each Mass, the Church always prays for the forgiveness of our sins.

**The Gospel story of the paralysed man**

When the four friends of the paralysed man in the Gospel story carried him to the house where Jesus was teaching, they couldn't get in because of the great crowd. St Luke says, "they went up on to the flat roof and lowered him and his stretcher down through the tiles into the middle of the gathering, in front of Jesus". What a dramatic entrance! Jesus was obviously deeply moved by the faith of the four friends. The Gospel says, "Seeing their faith, [Jesus] said, 'My friend, your sins are forgiven you'" (Luke 5:18-20). It is through the faith of the four friends that the paralysed man receives the gift of redemption, the forgiveness of his sins. Before he offered the paralysed man any other good gift, Jesus wanted to take away his sins. Jesus came among us to save us from our sins. But the Pharisees, the inveterate critics of Jesus, began to object, "Who can forgive sins but God alone?" This gave Jesus the opportunity to show them that he had the power to do both and he said to the paralysed man, "get up, and pick up your stretcher and go home" (Luke 5:21-24).

Jesus was not saying that it was sin that was the cause of the man's paralysis. In fact, when his disciples came across a man born blind, they asked him, "'Rabbi, who sinned, this man or his parents, for him to have been born blind?' 'Neither he nor his parents sinned,' Jesus answered" (John 9:1-3). He gave a similar answer to the people who told him about the Galileans whom Pilate had killed: "Do you suppose these Galileans who suffered like that were greater sinners than any other Galileans? They were not, I tell you. No; but unless you repent you will all perish as they did" (Luke 13:2-3). Sickness and misfortune are not inflicted by God as a punishment for sin. That is the constant teaching of Jesus. But many people still feel that if something bad happens to them, God is punishing them. This impedes that childlike trust that is so essential for true faith. Bad things, of course, do happen, but they are not caused by God. St Paul points out, "We know that by turning everything to their good God co-operates with all those who love him" (Romans 8:28). God brings good out of all evil.

In his 2014 message for the World Day of the Sick, Pope Francis wrote:

> The Church recognizes in you, the sick, a special presence of the suffering Christ. It is true. At the side of – and indeed within – our suffering, is the suffering of Christ; he bears its burden with us and he reveals its meaning. When the Son of God mounted the cross, he destroyed the solitude of suffering and illuminated its darkness. We thus find ourselves before the mystery of God's love for us, which gives us hope and courage: hope, because in the plan of God's love even the night of pain yields to the light of Easter, and courage, which enables us to confront every hardship in his company, in union with him.[6]

## The suffering Christ

After Jesus had given us the sacrament of his Body and Blood at the Last Supper, he went with his disciples to the garden of Gethsemane where he experienced great anguish of soul. He said to his chosen disciples: "My soul is sorrowful to the point of death." To God his Father he prayed: "My Father, if it is possible, let this cup pass me by. Nevertheless, let it be as you, not I, would have it" (Matthew 26:37-39). When St Luke recounts this scene of the Lord's suffering in the garden he tells us: "Then an angel appeared to him, coming from heaven to give him strength. In his anguish he prayed even more earnestly, and his sweat fell to the ground like great drops of blood" (Luke 22:43-44).

---

6   Message of Pope Francis for the 22nd World Day of the Sick 2014, 6 December 2013.

God heard the cry of Jesus. God the Father sent an angel, a messenger, bringing his own strength, to comfort him. God did not remove the cause of the agony, Jesus' approaching cruel crucifixion, but gave Jesus strength and power to go through his passion and death. His hour had come. He kept vigil in the garden until the Father sent him strength from heaven in the form of the angel. In all the suffering that ensued – his mock trial, his cruel scourging, his carrying of the cross, his agonising death – we see Jesus sustained by the strength of the Father as he overcame all the powers of evil.

**The mystery of evil**

For unbelievers, evil is just a cruel and disturbing fact of life; for believers, who believe in a loving and omnipotent God, evil is a mystery. The Catechism rightly reminds us that:

> We must therefore approach the question of the origin of evil by fixing the eyes of our faith on him who alone is its conqueror.[7]

We are the "fallen children of Adam". As St Paul says, "Sin entered the world through one man, and through sin death, and thus death has spread through the whole human race because everyone has sinned" (Romans 5:12). Christ, the New Adam, came "to undo all that the devil has done" (1 John 3:8) by giving "his life as a ransom for many" (Mark 10:45). Jesus, who overcame evil through the sacrifice of his life for our salvation, taught us to pray to the Father, "lead us not into temptation, but deliver us from evil".

In the great prayer for deliverance in Mass, after the Lord's Prayer, the first thing the Church prays is: "Deliver us, Lord, we pray, from every evil." Just before the priest receives Holy Communion he prays, "free me by this, your most holy Body and Blood, from all my sins and from every evil". Evil exists in our world and the Mass teaches us to earnestly pray to the Father to be delivered from all evil. We cannot overcome evil by our own strengths. It is only

---

7  *Catechism of the Catholic Church*, 385.

through Christ and through his redeeming love that we can resist and overcome evil. St John Paul II wrote in his encyclical letter on suffering:

> In the mystery of the Church as his Body, Christ has in a sense opened his own redemptive suffering to all human suffering. In so far as man becomes a sharer in Christ's suffering – in any part of the world and at any time in history – to that extent *he in his own way completes* the suffering through which Christ accomplished the Redemption of the world.[8]

We can speak, therefore, of "redemptive suffering". Human suffering in and by itself has no redemptive value. In fact, St John Paul II said, "Suffering is, in itself, an experience of evil." We fight against suffering in every way we can. But human suffering, patiently accepted and lovingly united to the suffering Christ, especially in the celebration of Mass, has a "redemptive value". St John Paul II explains:

> *It is [Christ]* – as the interior Master and Guide – *who reveals* to the suffering brother and sister this *wonderful interchange*, situated at the very heart of the mystery of the Redemption. Suffering is, in itself, an experience of evil. But Christ has made suffering the firmest basis of the definitive good, namely the good of eternal salvation. By his suffering on the Cross, Christ reached the very roots of evil, of sin and death. He conquered the author of evil, Satan, and his permanent rebellion against the Creator.[9]

During Mass, especially if we are labouring with sickness or suffering, we have to pray as Jesus prayed during his agony in Gethsemane, "Father, if it is possible, let this cup pass me by. Nevertheless, let it be as you, not I, would have it." We pray with total confidence that the Father hears and will bless us, just as he

---

8   John Paul II, *Salvifici Doloris*, 24.
9   Ibid., 26.

blessed Jesus in his agony. Without a renewed and a deepened faith, the sick person may not be able to accept what the Church recommends in time of sickness:

> The Church exhorts them [the sick] to associate themselves willingly with the passion and death of Christ (see Romans 8:17), and thus contribute to the welfare of the people of God.[10]

Indeed, the "sustaining of trust in God" is considered one of the effects of the sacrament of anointing.[11]

The *Catechism of the Catholic Church* develops this teaching on the sacrament in this way:

> By the grace of this sacrament the sick person receives the strength and the gift of uniting himself more closely to Christ's Passion: in a certain way he is consecrated to bear fruit by configuration to the Saviour's redemptive Passion. Suffering, a consequence of original sin, acquires a new meaning; it becomes a participation in the saving work of Jesus.[12]

While we pray many times during the Mass for healing, we do so in the spirit of Jesus' acceptance of God's will, by offering all our sickness, all our tears and suffering to the heavenly Father in the firm belief that he will bring good out of everything for us. In a beautiful image the psalmist tells us that God "collects [our] tears in [God's] wineskin" (Psalm 56:8). Every tear offered to God is treasured by God and will bring a blessing on you and on all you are praying for.

### The glory of God
We pray for healing in every Mass, but we do not offer the Mass for healing. We offer the Mass, in the first place, for the glory of

---

10 *Pastoral Care of the Sick*, General Introduction, 5.
11 Ibid., 6.
12 *Catechism of the Catholic Church*, 1521.

God. It is God who is at the centre of the Mass and it is God's right to glory and not our need for healing that is uppermost in the mind of the Church. There is, however, no conflict here. God's right to glory and our need for healing come together in a most marvellous way as we celebrate the Eucharist. St Irenaeus told us that the "glory of God is the human person fully alive". This means that when God is being glorified, something is happening in us. We are being changed. Everything in us that is in any way opposed to being fully alive in the Spirit is being dealt with. If it is a sin, it is being forgiven; if it is a wound of sin, it is being healed; if it is a bondage of sin or evil, we are being set free. God is glorified as we are changed, healed and freed.

During the celebration of the sacrament of reconciliation the priest says, in the prayer of absolution, that God has "sent the Holy Spirit among us for the forgiveness of sins". This teaches us to see the forgiveness of our sins as the special work of the Spirit. The Catechism teaches us in this way:

> Healing the wounds of sin, the Holy Spirit renews us interiorly through a spiritual transformation. He enlightens and strengthens us to live as "children of light" through "all that is good and right and true".[13]

The wounds of sins are not just the wounds that we inflict on ourselves when we sin. They are also, and most often, the wounds that the sins of others against us inflict on us. We bring these wounds to the Mass. We offer them to God as we offer the bread and wine, the symbols of our offering that we are making of ourselves, in union with the offering that Christ is making of himself. For instance, if you are in a stressful relationship, at home or at work, from which you cannot escape at present, always try to offer up all the hurt and pain you are experiencing to God during the Mass. And try to do that without engaging in judgement or

---

13 *Catechism of the Catholic Church*, 1695.

condemnation of those involved. This is where you need the Holy Spirit to heal the wounds of sin that are being inflicted on you. As you open your heart to receive this healing, you are being justified. Again, the Catechism offers these words of comfort for us when it speaks of justification:

> Justification is not only the remission of sins, but also the renewal of the interior man… It frees from the enslavement to sin, and it heals… Justification establishes *cooperation between God's grace and man's freedom*.[14]

God liberates our freedom so that we can freely choose to do what is right and good.

### Forgive us as we forgive them

The Lord's Prayer comes at a key moment in the celebration of the Mass. It is like our "grace before the Eucharistic banquet", before we partake of the banquet of "the living bread that has come down from heaven". In that prayer we ask God to "forgive us our trespasses, as we forgive those who trespass against us". In Chapter Five we considered the implications of this condition, "as we forgive", in some detail. We will now look at some scientific evidence about the healing power of forgiving. Jesus said that he came "so that they might have life and have it to the full" (John 10:10). He asks us to do what is necessary to receive this "life to the full". When St Peter asked him how often he should forgive, Jesus said, "seventy-seven times" (Matthew 18:22). In other words, Jesus is asking us to forgive unconditionally. Since his desire for us is that we "have life to the full" it should not surprise us to discover that the "seventy-seven times" forgiveness is the very best thing we can do for our own health. Jesus practised this kind of forgiveness himself. On the cross he prayed for his executioners, "Father, forgive them; they do not know what they are doing" (Luke 23:34). His forgiveness of them did not depend on their

---

14 Ibid., 1989-1990, 1993.

repentance, but without their repentance his generosity would not change their hearts.

Filled with God's love and with God's Spirit, we are moved to offer to others what God has given us: unconditional forgiveness. Forgiveness is the work of the Spirit. Christ's forgiveness comes to us in the Spirit and our forgiveness of others goes to them in the Spirit. St Paul says: "Since the Spirit is our life, let us be directed by the Spirit" (Galatians 5:25). For the Christian, forgiveness is a mark of our reconciliation with God. But forgiveness does not require social reconciliation between offender and victim, since it can be offered to the unrepentant as much as the repentant.[15] In Mass we are invited to cope with the stress caused by "the wounds of sin" inflicted by others through forgiveness and offering the sign of peace. This is the surest way of healing the broken heart.

**Science rediscovers the healing power of forgiveness**
Stanford University in California carried out detailed research on how forgiving improves health. They invited five women who had suffered the loss of either their husband or son through the violence in Northern Ireland. When they arrived, broken-hearted, at Stanford, they had a medical check-up before they were invited to enter into a week of training on forgiving. At the end of the week's training they had another medical check-up. Six months later, back in Belfast, they had another medical check-up. These are some of the health findings:

> On the measure of how hurt the Irish women felt by their loss, on a scale of 1 to 10, they began the week with a score of 8.5.

> When they left at the end of the week, they registered their hurt a bit over 3.5. When the questionnaires were returned at the six-month follow-up, their hurt score still stood below 4.

---

15 For a detailed study of the health benefits of forgiving from the heart see Jim McManus and Stephanie Thornton, *Finding Forgiveness* (Chawton: Redemptorist Publications, 2005).

The women reduced stress by almost half from the beginning of the training to the follow-up six months later.

An increase of forgiveness by forty per cent towards those who had killed their loved ones.

Given a list of thirty items indicating depression, the women checked an average of seventeen at the beginning, an average of seven at the end of the training, and ten at the six-month follow-up.

The women also showed that by the follow-up assessment they had become significantly more optimistic.[16]

Those who believe that we live by every word that comes from the mouth of God are not surprised by these findings. Jesus asks us to forgive "seventy-seven times" and therefore we believe that there can be nothing better for the health of the heart than to forgive from the heart. The double sadness in those who do not forgive from the heart is that they continue to carry the hurt inflicted when the offence was committed, and each day they relive that hurt by ruminating on it. Those women from Northern Ireland began their exploration of forgiving with an average of seventeen symptoms indicating depression. At the end of the week these symptoms were reduced to seven. Forgiving not only heals the wounds of sin but it also lifts the spirit and infuses the joy of the Spirit.

In our celebration of the Mass we receive the grace to forgive from the heart as we say the Lord's Prayer. This grace heals the broken heart and brings great peace and joy. If you have a deep hurt in your life you should always bring it to Mass, offer it to God and open your heart to receive the healing that comes through forgiveness. You will certainly receive that healing if you are willing to forgive. And, to encourage yourself to forgive, you could remind yourself frequently that by harbouring bitterness and resentment you are hurting only yourself.

---

16 For full details of the Stanford research see Dr Fred Luskin, *Forgive for Good* (San Francisco: Harper, 2002).

## Safe from all distress

The priest prays in the prayer for deliverance, after the Lord's Prayer, that we shall be kept "safe from all distress, as we await the blessed hope and the coming of our Saviour, Jesus Christ". It is necessary to pray that prayer with great confidence, resisting all doubts about God's love and care. To be kept safe from distress is a great healing. But if we hold on to our worries, we cannot be protected from them by God. God never forces our freedom. God the Father invites us to allow him to take care of all our fears, anxieties and worries. He assures us in scripture that he is our rock, our protection, our stronghold, our deliverer. But he awaits our free cooperation. Just as Jesus had to say to the man by the pool, "Do you want to be well again?" (John 5:6), so he says to us, "Do you want to be protected from all your stressful anxieties? Do you want to let go of your worries?" If we do, then the Lord will most certainly keep us "safe from all distress". Stress can cause many manifestations of illness. Herbert Benson, professor of medicine at Harvard Medical School, wrote:

> Sixty to ninety percent of visits to physicians are for conditions related to stress. Harmful effects of stress include anxiety, mild and moderate depression, anger and hostility, hypertension, pain, insomnia and many other stress-related diseases.[17]

Recall that those Irish women in the Stanford Forgiveness Project "reduced stress by almost half from the beginning of the training to the follow-up six months later". When the Church prays during Mass for God to keep us safe from all distress, she is asking for a multiple healing for us. This is the time to present all stressful circumstances to God. We have to be careful to resist engaging in condemnations of others in our prayers.

We combine this prayer for protection against distress with another request to God, namely, that "we may be always be free from sin".

---

17 Herbert Benson, *The Relaxation Response* (New York: Quill, 2000), p. 1.

Nothing causes more distress to the human spirit than deliberate sin. Sin puts self before God; cuts self off from God; and leaves self feeling all alone in the spiritual world where the human spirit seeks meaning and purpose in life. God never abandons us in our sins. That is why we never fail to pray for forgiveness throughout the Mass. We need the grace of repentance in our heart and we need to come to "the Lamb of God who takes away the sins of the world" and humbly ask him to take away all our sins. Once we sincerely seek the Lord, we will find him.

**Peace I leave with you**

After the prayer for deliverance the priest says this beautiful prayer, reminding us that Jesus came to bring us peace:

> Lord Jesus Christ,
> who said to your Apostles:
> Peace I leave you, my peace I give you,
> look not on our sins,
> but on the faith of your Church,
> and graciously grant her peace and unity
> in accordance with your will.

We open our hearts to receive this wonderful gift of peace from Christ. Like the gift of forgiveness, peace is a gift that we have to share with others. If we do not share it with others we will not be able to hold on to it for ourselves. Benedict XVI expressed this well when he wrote:

> Union with Christ is also union with all those to whom he gives himself. I cannot possess Christ just for myself; I can belong to him only in union with all those who have become, or who will become, his own.[18]

When the priest or deacon says to us, "Let us offer each other the sign of peace," nobody can be excluded from this sign. Because

---

18 Benedict XVI, *Sacramentum Caritatis*, 89.

peace is first of all Christ's gift to us, we have to share it with everyone if we want to experience it for ourselves.

### Specific prayers for healing in the Eucharist

For the past fifteen hundred years, in the Roman Canon of the Mass, the priest has prayed "for the redemption of their souls, in hope of health and well-being" of all present. Before receiving Holy Communion he prays silently; the Missal gives two alternative prayers, one of which is:

> May the receiving of your Body and Blood,
> Lord Jesus Christ,
> not bring me to judgement and condemnation,
> but through your loving mercy
> be for me protection in mind and body
> and a healing remedy.

And just before receiving he invites all the people to join in saying,

> Lord, I am not worthy
> that you should enter under my roof,
> but only say the word
> and my soul shall be healed.

"My soul" means "my whole being, my innermost self". While purifying the chalice after Communion, he continues to pray for healing:

> What has passed our lips as food, O Lord,
> may we possess in purity of heart,
> that what has been given to us in time
> may be our healing for eternity.

Some of the Prayers after Communion have very specific requests for healing. These beautiful prayers are the last prayers of the Mass and very often we don't pay close attention to them. The Prayer after Communion generally consists of two parts. In the first part we thank God for the grace of the Eucharist that we have just celebrated, and in the second part we ask that this Eucharist will affect some very specific area of our life.

For example, on the Monday of the first week of Lent, this is how the Church gives thanks for the Eucharist and requests healing:

> We pray, O Lord, that, in receiving your Sacrament,
> we may experience help in mind and body
> so that, kept safe in both,
> we may glory in the fullness of heavenly healing.

The request in this prayer is very daring. We pray to "experience help in mind and body". It is one thing to have a theoretical knowledge of God's love. It is quite another thing to experience God's healing love and to expect to "glory in the fullness of heavenly healing". To say this prayer with faith we must open our whole being to God and allow the healing love of God to fill us, removing all barriers. We open our minds and submit to the all-holy God and allow the presence of God's healing Spirit to renew and transform our minds. We surrender all care and worry, all fear and doubt, and we invite God to renew us. But too often our prayer is half-hearted. We want to be healed, but we don't want to trust; we want to be protected from anxiety, but we want to hold on to our worries; we want to forgive from the heart, but we also want to get our own back in some way.

Consider another Prayer after Communion:

> We pray, O Lord our God,
> that, as you have given these most sacred mysteries
> to be the safeguard of our salvation,
> so you may make them a healing remedy for us,
> both now and in time to come.[19]

---

19 Prayer after Communion, Thursday of the first week of Lent.

Notice the word "now" in that prayer. The Church wants something to happen *now*, not tomorrow, not next week, but now! It is now, in this hour, that we need to know the healing presence of God. Just before Christmas, in the Mass of 21 December, this is how the Church prays:

> Lord, may participation in this divine mystery
> provide enduring protection for your people,
> so that, being subject to your glorious majesty
>     in dedicated service,
> they may know abundant health in mind and body.

Finally, consider the Collect of one of the Masses in honour of Our Lady:

> Grant, Lord God, that we, your servants,
> may rejoice in unfailing health of mind and body,
> and, through the glorious intercession
>     of Blessed Mary ever-Virgin,
> may we be set free from present sorrow
> and come to enjoy eternal happiness.[20]

That request for "unfailing health of mind and body", through the intercession of Our Lady, should give us great confidence as we pray for healing at Mass.

All these prayers for healing within the Mass indicate how strongly the Church believes in God's healing love, and how she expects that healing power to be experienced in the Mass. Does our faith correspond to the faith of the Church? Do we believe as strongly in divine healing? Do we "attune our minds to our voices" as we say these prayers? With so many prayers for the healing of body, mind and spirit in the Mass, isn't it extraordinary that, for so long, we didn't allow these prayers to form an expectant faith in God's healing love in us and inform our theology and our catechetical

---

20 Common of the Blessed Virgin Mary in Ordinary Time, 1.

instruction on the Mass? Had we acted consistently on the old maxim, "The way the Church prays manifests what the Church believes," we would have no difficulty in accepting the healing ministry in our time. But sadly, I fear, we over-spiritualised the meaning of these prayers and thought that they were just referring to helping the soul get to heaven. While we always expected the forgiveness of sins, we didn't always expect the healing of the wounds of sin, the healing of body, mind and spirit.

In the past, of course, all those beautiful prayers for healing were said silently or in Latin. We can understand all the prayers of the Mass today. As we celebrate the Mass, however, we have to keep reminding ourselves of the truth so well expressed by the Second Vatican Council:

> In order that the liturgy may be able to produce its full results it is necessary that the faithful come to it with proper dispositions, that their minds be attuned to their voices, that they cooperate with heavenly grace lest they receive it in vain.[21]

---

21 *Sacrosanctum Concilium*, Constitution on the Sacred Liturgy, 11.

# Chapter Eight

# Go and announce the Gospel of the Lord

During the Mass we celebrate the good news that Jesus Christ our Saviour is risen from the dead and that he wants us to receive his great gift of redemption from all our sins. We don't keep this good news to ourselves. One form of the words with which we are sent forth at the end of the Mass reminds us of this: "Go and announce the Gospel of the Lord." The Mass is never for oneself alone, nor for one's community alone. The Mass is for the whole world. And the "Go" that we hear as we are sent forth from the Mass echoes Christ's final word to the disciples just before he ascended to heaven, "Go out to the world; proclaim the Good News" (Mark 16:16). Those first disciples of Jesus, transformed by the Holy Spirit, did that. They went forth and preached the good news: Jesus Christ, risen from the dead, is the Saviour of the whole human race. Many believed their message. The Church of Christ had made its appearance in history. For the past two thousand years the Church of Christ has been present in our world because disciples, men and women, have continued to act on the command of Jesus, "Go", and they have gone throughout the length and breadth of their countries and across the entire word to bring the good news of redemption.

Now it is our turn to act on that "Go" with which Jesus sends us. We are in his company during the Mass. He is there to meet us when we enter into the sacred assembly of the gathering congregation. He speaks to us as the scriptures are being proclaimed. He unites our offering of ourselves to the Father with the perfect offering that he makes of himself, so that we can share in his perfect sacrifice. And, as our gifts of bread and wine are transformed into his own Body and Blood, he gives us himself in Holy Communion. We are most intimately united with Jesus, our brother, the Son of God, and it is now he who sends us forth with the divine command, "Go and announce the good news."

This command is given to the whole community and not just to individuals. It is as a community that we must respond. After Mass we don't cease to be a community. We keep our community dimension and awareness all the time. In the world of football, if the team "loses its shape", if it ceases to really play as a team, it will never win. We, the congregation of the Lord, have to "play as the Lord's team", keeping our shape as a "Eucharistic community" even when we are on our own.

## Deepest identity of the Church

Our first duty as a Eucharistic community is to bring the good news of Christ and his redemption to others. When we do this we are embracing our deepest identity as the Church of Christ. Blessed Paul VI wrote:

> Evangelizing is in fact the grace and vocation proper to the Church, her deepest identity. She exists in order to evangelize, that is to say, in order to preach and teach, to be the channel of the gift of grace, to reconcile sinners with God, and to perpetuate Christ's sacrifice in the Mass, which is the memorial of his death and glorious resurrection.[1]

The Church exists for those who have not yet heard the good news that Jesus Christ has redeemed them: he is calling them into a personal relationship with himself; he wants them to experience the full forgiveness of their sins; his one desire is for each person to be filled with the Holy Spirit. Each time we go to Mass we celebrate this mystery of redemption. We also assume our deepest identity as Church. Our deepest identity, the identity we share with one another as members of the Church, is that we are called to

---

1  Paul VI, *Evangelii Nuntiandi*, 14.

bring the good news of Christ to others, to evangelise. Each parish community has to sincerely ask itself this question: How are we as a Eucharistic community living our deepest identity through evangelising?

## A missionary Church

We have always identified as missionaries those who left their homeland and were sent to bring the Gospel of Christ to people who had not yet heard of him. St Patrick came back to Ireland as a missionary to convert the Irish. Ss Augustine, Columba and Aidan are honoured as the great missionaries to Scotland and England. St Boniface, an Anglo-Saxon missionary, is honoured as one of the patron saints of Germany. In the sixth, seventh and eighth centuries, monks from Ireland went all over Europe to preach the Gospel. While the great European powers – Britain, Spain, France, Germany, Belgium, Holland and Portugal – were colonising North and South America, Australia and New Zealand and Africa, and establishing their overseas empires from the sixteenth century onwards, tens of thousands of men and women joined missionary orders and congregations and were sent to those new colonies to preach the Gospel. Those missionaries from Europe planted the Church throughout Africa and Asia, in Australasia and the Americas. It is a story of great faith and heroism, of dedication and total commitment.

Catholic parishes and parishioners were always most generous in the way they supported their overseas missionaries. But, instead of seeing themselves as missionaries in their own local area, those great benefactors of the overseas missionaries saw themselves simply in a support role to the "real missionaries". As good disciples of Christ, they practised their Catholic faith, went to Mass, said their prayers and supported their Church. The work of evangelising belonged to the professionals, the priests and the men and women of Religious Orders. The ordinary laity, who stayed at home and reared their families, were not encouraged to see themselves as missionaries or evangelisers. This resulted in many good, practising Catholics not feeling that it was their responsibility as members of their parish, their Eucharistic community, to "spread the faith". A survey carried out among Catholics in the USA revealed these rather disturbing statistics:

> Asked whether spreading the faith was a high priority of their parishes, 75 percent of American Protestant congregations and 57 percent of African American congregations responded affirmatively, whereas 6 percent of Catholic parishes did the same. Asked whether they sponsored local evangelistic activities, 39 percent of conservative Protestant congregations and 16 percent of African American congregations responded positively as compared with only 3 percent of Catholic parishes.[2]

These are troubling findings. We are sent forth from the Mass with the specific mandate to "Go and announce the Gospel of the Lord," to tell others about the redemption we all need and find through Jesus Christ and about the friendship that he wishes to have with each of us. We were given the peace of Christ to share with one another during the Mass and to share with others after the Mass. As parish communities we have a duty to do this. In fact, St John Paul II said:

> No Christian community is faithful to its duty unless it is missionary: either it is a *missionary community* or it is not even a *Christian community*, because these are simply two dimensions of the same reality, which is brought about by baptism and the other sacraments.[3]

The challenge to the ordinary Catholic parish today is to become a missionary parish. During a parish mission I always spell out as

---

2  Avery Cardinal Dulles, Foreword, in Timothy E. Byerley, *The Great Commission* (Mahwah, NJ: Paulist Press, 2008).
3  John Paul II, Message for World Mission Day, 20 October 1991.

clearly as I can that the purpose of the parish mission is to enable a practising parish to become an evangelising parish. This is the conversion that good Catholic parishes need, to move from just "practising" the faith to spreading the faith. In the words of St John Paul II:

> A radical conversion of thinking is required in order to become missionary, and this holds true both for individuals and entire communities.[4]

Your parish community, its priest and people, whom you join each Sunday to celebrate Mass, may be in need of this "radical conversion of thinking". Notice it is not a moral conversion, or a religious conversion, but a conversion of the way in which we see ourselves as Church, as disciples to whom Christ says, "Go out to the whole world; proclaim the Good News to all creation" (Mark 16:16). How do we accept this great commission from Jesus to be his evangelisers in our time?

**Missionary disciples**

The "radical conversion" that St John Paul II spoke about involves changing the way we see our lives: our relationship with God in Christ; our relationship with our Christian community; our relationship with the whole non-believing world around us. Pope Francis expresses this very clearly when he writes:

> In virtue of their baptism, all the members of the People of God have become missionary disciples (cf. Matthew 28:19). All the baptized, whatever their position in the Church or their level of instruction in the faith, are agents of evangelization, and it would be insufficient to envisage a plan of evangelization carried out by professionals while the rest of the faithful would simply be passive recipients. The new evangelization calls for personal involvement on

---

4   John Paul II, *Redemptoris Missio*, 49.

the part of each of the baptized… we no longer say that we are "disciples" and "missionaries", but rather that we are always "missionary disciples".[5]

We have to begin to think of ourselves as "missionary disciples" and ask ourselves how we are living our "deepest identity" in our local Christian communities. We can never live out our missionary vocation in isolation from our faith community. We pray at Mass to be "gathered into one by the Holy Spirit".[6] We don't abandon that unity once Mass is over. We take a "Eucharistic outlook" with us from the celebration of the Mass. As St John Paul II said:

> Proclaiming the death of the Lord "until he comes" (1 Corinthians 11:26) entails that all who take part in the Eucharist be committed to changing their lives and making them in a certain way completely "Eucharistic".[7]

St Paul said, "As there is one loaf, so we, although there are many of us, are one single body, for we all share in the one loaf" (1 Corinthians 10:17). We live the "Eucharistic life" when we gratefully and consciously maintain this awareness of our "Eucharistic unity". We are brothers and sisters in Christ. The Holy Eucharist is called the "sacrament of love". At Mass we celebrate the mystery of Christ's redeeming love for us. As he himself said, "No one can have greater love than to lay down his life for his friends. You are my friends, if you do what I command you" (John 15:13-14). We enter into the mystery of this love in the Mass. It is in and through his redeeming love that we become "one body, one spirit in Christ". We leave the church at the end of Mass united in this love of Christ. The "Eucharistic life" that we continue to live is a manifestation of the Church. As the Second Vatican Council said, the Church is "a people made one by the unity of the Father, the Son and the Holy Spirit".[8]

---

5  Pope Francis, *Evangelii Gaudium*, 120.
6  Eucharistic Prayer II.
7  John Paul II, *Ecclesia de Eucharistia*, 20.
8  *Lumen Gentium*, Dogmatic Constitution on the Church, 4.

## Living the Eucharistic life

Living the Eucharistic life inoculates us against the virus of pessimism. We proclaim in the Mass that we "await the blessed hope and the coming of our Saviour, Jesus Christ". This joyful hope can imbue us with serene confidence in the face of the challenges that we have to face in life because we believe that Christ has "conquered the world" (John 16:33). Significantly Pope Francis quotes the opening address of St John XXIII to the Second Vatican Council on 11 October 1962 to show us how we have to face the challenges before us today. St John XXIII said:

> At times we have to listen, much to our regret, to the voices of people, who though burning with zeal, lack a sense of discretion and measure. In this modern age they can see nothing but prevarication and ruin... We feel that we must disagree with those prophets of doom who are always forecasting disaster, as though the end of the world were at hand. In our times, divine Providence is leading us to a new order of human relations which, by human effort and even beyond all expectations, are directed to the fulfilment of God's superior and inscrutable designs, in which everything, even human setbacks, leads to the greater good of the Church.[9]

The prophets of doom can see only what is wrong with the Church and the world and can never rejoice in seeing the seeds of new life that sprout up in every age. They are mesmerised by "human setbacks". Although they are zealous in many ways, the pessimists that St John XXIII complained about are not really living in joyful hope, nor does their pessimism about life make them ready to welcome Christ when he comes again. I often think that their first words to him will probably be, "Why did it take you so long?" or "So you decided to come back, at last!" That pessimistic outlook on life is the opposite of the Eucharistic outlook.

---

9  John XXIII, Address for the Opening of the Second Vatican Council, cited in Pope Francis, *Evangelii Gaudium*, 84.

We are sent forth from our Sunday celebration of Mass, not to retreat back into an individualistic existence, concerned only for ourselves, but to announce, both by the way we live our lives, and with our words, the good news that Jesus Christ is risen from the dead, that he lives with us, forgives all our sins and heals every wound of sin. Reflect on the confidence with which the Church says this prayer during Mass:

> O God, who restore human nature
> to yet greater dignity than at its beginnings,
> look upon the amazing mystery of your loving kindness,
> and in those you have chosen to make new
> through the wonder of rebirth
> may you preserve the gifts
> of your enduring grace and blessing.[10]

That is not the prayer of a pessimist or a defeatist. Pope Francis warns against the paralysing power of defeatism:

> The evil spirit of defeatism is brother to the temptation to separate, before its time, the wheat from the weeds; it is the fruit of an anxious and self-centred lack of trust.[11]

### Give a reason for the hope that is in you

Living the Eucharistic life enables us live each day in joyful hope. The vast majority of people who become Catholics say that it was the example of an individual Catholic, often a friendly neighbour who always had a smile and a kind word for them, that set them on the road to the Church. They became curious and began to suspect that this kind person had the "secret of happiness" because, no matter what he or she had to come through, that person never lost his or her inner peace and joy. Sooner or later they take the step of asking him or her, "What is your secret? Why do you always look peaceful and joyful?" This is the situation that St Peter had

---

10 Collect for Thursday after the Fourth Sunday of Easter.
11 Pope Francis, *Evangelii Gaudium*, 85.

in mind when he wrote, "Simply reverence the Lord Christ in your hearts, and always have your answer ready for people who ask you the reason for the hope that you all have. But give it with courtesy and respect…" (1 Peter 3:15-16). When people ask you the secret of your peace you will be able to tell them that it is not because you have good, psychological, coping skills but because you have received peace as a gift from Christ. Indeed, you could say with St Paul that "[Christ] is the peace between us" (Ephesians 2:14). You could also say that you firmly believe that Christ wants each person to have his peace. If you have been able to say something like that to people, you have planted a seed of faith that will grow.

### The Church grows by attraction
Pope Francis writes:

> It is not by proselytizing that the Church grows, but "by attraction".[12]

In our society, where people are not united by cultural or racial or sometimes even family ties, the warmth, hospitality and unity of the Catholic community make a deep impression. Why are such a diverse group of people no longer strangers to each other? This gives a powerful witness to Christ. The joyful, warm and welcoming parish community is the Church's greatest asset for evangelisation. Sometimes, however, this witness can be greatly undermined by divisions and cliques and indifference towards one another. During a parish mission, in a very large parish, I met a lady who had recently lapsed from the practice of her faith. She was very angry. What she said to me then has remained with me ever since. She said, "The thing that hurts me most is that I am not even missed!" Nobody knew she was there, nobody noticed she was not there. Her presence or absence made no difference to that community. As a consequence, she never felt that she belonged or that she was accepted as a sister to everyone else at Mass. As a result, she lapsed

---

12 *Evangelii Gaudium*, 15.

from the practice of her faith. I got a real insight into how the faith of the individual can be at risk in a large, anonymous congregation. Is it a loving, welcoming, caring community, or is it composed of groups of friends or small cliques that don't want to be bothered with someone they don't know? The testimony of this woman confirmed for me the findings of an investigation in the 1980s, carried out in every Catholic diocese in the world at the request of the Vatican, on why Catholics leave their parishes to join other churches, usually the Pentecostal or house churches. What are they searching for? The survey discovered that the very first thing they are looking for is a warm, welcoming community, where they are known, where their gifts are recognised and used.[13] When they find such a community they usually stay there at least for a few years.

In the Mass we pray to become "one body, one spirit in Christ". We pray for the gift of true communion with Christ and with one another. Our communion with Christ and with one another doesn't cease as we leave the church. The ultimate norm of good liturgy, a good celebration of the Mass, is not how the congregation sings and participates in the prayer, but how they relate to each other, especially as they are leaving the church. If we have become "one body, one spirit in Christ" in the celebration of the mystery of our faith, that unity should still keep us united as brothers and sisters as we leave the church and return to our homes. In fact, that unity remains and becomes visible again next time we assemble to celebrate the Mass. If the unity were to evaporate the moment the Mass is over, what kind of unity would it be? Was that gift of unity ever gratefully accepted?

## A spirituality of communion

To protect and foster this unity we need to live what St John Paul II called "a spirituality of communion". In his great vision for the Church as we entered the new millennium he wrote,

---

13 See Vatican Report, *Sects or New Religious Movements: A Pastoral Challenge*, May 1986.

> To make the Church *the home and the school of communion*:
> that is the great challenge facing us in the millennium
> which is now beginning, if we wish to be faithful to God's
> plan and respond to the world's deepest yearnings.[14]

The deepest yearning in the human heart is to belong to the human
community. That yearning is placed there by God. As the Second
Vatican Council teaches:

> [God] willed to make women and men holy and to save
> them, not as individuals without any bond between
> them, but rather to make them into a people who might
> acknowledge him and serve him in holiness.[15]

Spiritually we are bonded together. That is why we need to cultivate
a spirituality of communion: we see ourselves as brothers and
sisters in the Lord; we live out our relationship in love, peace and
generosity with all the members of our parish; we share the love
that God puts in our hearts in the celebration of the Eucharist with
everyone. As St John Paul II said:

> A spirituality of communion implies also the ability to see
> what is positive in others, to welcome it and prize it as a
> gift from God: not only as a gift for the brother or sister
> who has received it directly, but also as a "gift for me".[16]

In the parish community we all have our different gifts. In Mass
we are grateful to God for all these gifts. We give thanks to God
"that you have held us worthy to be in your presence and minister
to you".[17] In this prayer we are thanking God, not just for the gifts
God has given to us as individuals, but for all the gifts that others
have received. A most destructive attitude towards the gifts of
others is jealousy, the refusal to rejoice in another person's gifts.
Since we pray to become "one body, one spirit in Christ", then the
gifts that God has given to other members of the body of Christ are,

---

14 John Paul II, *Novo Millennio Ineunte*, 43.

15 *Lumen Gentium*, 9.

16 John Paul II, *Novo Millennio Ineunte*, 43.

17 Eucharistic Prayer II.

as St John Paul II said, "a gift for me". Jealousy undermines the communion that binds the community together.

Living this spirituality of communion gives us the energy and conviction to live as "missionary disciples". Our Sunday or daily celebration of the Mass is where we feast at the "table of the word of God" and at the "table of the Body of the Lord". This is where our spirituality of communion is fostered, deepened and renewed. And it is from the Mass that the community is sent forth to announce the good news of Jesus Christ. The more the community remains united, by living and sharing a healthy spirituality of communion, the more effectively its members become "missionary disciples".

### The practising parish becomes an evangelising parish
The average Catholic parish engages in many good works and supports many good causes all over the world. We have always had great Catholic organisations, like the St Vincent de Paul Society, the Catholic Women's League, the Union of Catholic Mothers, the Legion of Mary, and many other outstanding groups of the faithful who give their time, energy and money to doing all kinds of good works and responding to all kinds of social needs. Some of these organisations, like the Legion of Mary, have always had evangelisation as a primary goal. Today all organisations within the parish have to live up to their missionary mandate. St John Paul II gave us a missionary criterion for assessing the effectiveness of our parochial or diocesan organisations:

> The effectiveness of the Church's organisations, movements, parishes and apostolic works must be measured in the light of this missionary imperative. Only by becoming missionary will the Christian community be able to overcome its internal divisions and tensions, and rediscover its unity and its strength of faith.[18]

---

18 John Paul II, *Redemptoris Missio*, 49.

Our missionary goal today is to ensure that our good, practising parishes become evangelising parishes. That is, the parish community today cannot be content with just "going to Mass" and contributing to collections for good causes. The parish is responsible for the evangelisation of all its members and those who are not yet believers.

Many good Catholics, when reminded that they are also evangelisers as well as practitioners of the faith, respond by saying that they have no training in theology or Catholic doctrine and so they are not equipped for this kind of work. Pope Francis has this understandable feeling of not being prepared in mind when he says:

> All the baptized, whatever their position in the Church or their level of instruction in the faith, are agents of evangelization, and it would be insufficient to envisage a plan of evangelization carried out by professionals while the rest of the faithful would simply be passive recipients.[19]

It is not the level of instruction that prepares us for this work, but the depth of our faith. However, as Pope Francis also points out, "In all its activities the parish encourages and trains its members to be evangelizers."[20] You may well ask yourself, "What encouragement or training have I been offered by my parish?" And, if that encouragement and training are not available at present, when will they become available? Who will take the initiative to make that training available?

I heard an American parish priest sharing with a group how his parish became active on all fronts. When he arrived as parish priest people came to him and asked, "Could we have this hour of prayer, or Bible study, or lectio divina, or rosary, or prayer group, or holy hour?" To each person or group he said, "This is your church, it is not mine. I am just the pastor. If you want this hour, take

19 Pope Francis, *Evangelii Gaudium*, 120.
20 Ibid., 28.

responsibility for it, organise it, advertise it, and I will help in any way I can but I will not lead it and I might not even be there." He released the initiative in all those groups and now they are making a great contribution to the vitality of the whole parish. That is good leadership.

**The faith *which we believe* and the faith *by which we believe***
Evangelisation is, in the first place, sharing one's faith with others. We use the word "faith" with two quite distinct meanings. We talk about the faith *which we believe*. That is the *doctrine* of the faith, which we can study for a lifetime. Theology is the science that studies doctrine. Not too many of us are theologians. And very often the best theologians are not the best evangelisers. We also talk about the faith *by which we believe*. This is the inner light, the conviction that enables us to say, "Yes, Lord, I believe that you are the Christ, the Son of the living God." That is the gift of faith. It is in and through this light of faith that we discover the meaning and purpose of our lives.

The Holy Spirit enables us to share this inner light with someone who is seeking the meaning and purpose of his or her life. This sharing is often quite spontaneous. We share faith in the same way that we share any other good news. For instance, if someone is sharing with you the trouble he or she is having, a gentle remark like "Without my faith in God I would find it very difficult to come through that kind of upset" can lift the sharing onto a new level. Before the person is fully aware of the new direction of the conversation, he or she may be asking you how your faith helped you. Then you have the opportunity to share your faith in Christ, share the relationship that you have with Christ, and introduce the person to the awareness that, at least for you, Jesus Christ is a friend at your side all the time. I had a boyhood friend who became an acute alcoholic in London as a young man. His wife and children were having a very hard time living with him. He was, in fact, in imminent danger of losing them. He told me that when this truth began to dawn on him he went up into the attic of his house, prostrated himself on the floor and cried out, "Christ, if you are there, you have to do something for me." Suddenly, he said, he seemed to be surrounded by light. He was filled with peace, freed from fear, confusion and anxiety, and never touched another drop of alcohol for the rest of his life. His marriage was saved. Not only that, he shared his story with everyone, especially with those who were afflicted with alcoholism or some other form of addiction. He became a committed "missionary disciple" and found great joy in helping others. As he shared his wonderful liberation story with me he was evangelising me, filling me with great joy and gratitude to Christ our Lord. Pope Francis describes him well:

> A committed missionary knows the joy of being a spring which spills over and refreshes others. Only the person who feels happiness in seeking the good of others, in desiring their happiness, can be a missionary. This openness of heart is a source of joy, since "it is more blessed to give than to receive" (Acts 20:35).[21]

When we share "the faith by which we believe" we are witnessing to the presence of Christ in our lives. My friend, when he told his story about crying out to Christ to do something for him, was not theologically trained but he gave great witness to Christ. Benedict XVI wrote:

> We become witnesses when, through our actions, words and way of being, Another makes himself present.[22]

The "Another" who becomes present is, of course, Christ himself. We then have the opportunity to introduce the person to Christ, to make Christ known. That is the heart of all evangelisation. When

---

21 *Evangelii Gaudium*, 272.
22 Benedict XVI, *Sacramentum Caritatis*, 85

we introduce the person to Jesus Christ we have done all we can. Now the Lord himself takes over.

We are sent forth from the Mass with the words, "Go and announce the Gospel of the Lord." This doesn't have to be done in a lot of words. Indeed, St Francis of Assisi used to say to his friars as he sent them out, "Go and preach the Gospel, and use words if necessary." St John Paul II emphasised this approach when he wrote:

> The first form of witness is *the very life of the missionary, of the Christian family*, and *of the ecclesial community*, which reveal a new way of living.[23]

We become evangelisers when we begin to live our Christian faith with joy and confidence in God's presence with us. People searching for a deeper meaning in their life begin to notice and to ask themselves, "Why are those people so happy?" It is the witness of their lives that attracts. Blessed Paul VI said it well when he wrote:

> For the Church, the first means of evangelization is the witness of an authentically Christian life, given over to God in a communion that nothing should destroy and at the same time given to one's neighbour with limitless zeal... Modern people listen more willingly to witnesses than to teachers, and if they do listen at all to teachers, it is because they are first witnesses.[24]

**What will I say?**
People can be fearful that, if they begin to share their own faith with someone, they will not be able to find the words to explain their experience of living the Catholic life and what celebrating the sacraments, especially the Mass, means to them. We should all take Blessed Paul VI's encouraging and inspiring words to heart:

> Evangelization will never be possible without the action of the Holy Spirit... It is the Holy Spirit who, today just as

---

23 John Paul II, *Redemptoris Missio*, 42.
24 Paul VI, *Evangelii Nuntiandi*, 41.

at the beginning of the Church, acts in every evangelizer who allows himself or herself to be possessed and led by him. The Holy Spirit places on their lips the words which they could not find by themselves, and at the same time the Holy Spirit predisposes the soul of the hearer to be open and receptive to the Good News and to the kingdom being proclaimed.[25]

The moment you find yourself with the opportunity to share your faith with someone, you are not alone. Christ is now with you. It is he who has brought about this moment. The Holy Spirit is within you and also within the person to whom you are speaking. It is the Spirit who will give you the words that will resonate in the other person's heart and reveal something of the mystery of God to him or her. On the surface it may seem to be a simple conversation, but it is all happening in the marvellous providence of God. We have to be confident and humble in God's presence as we share what the Lord has done in our own lives.

### The Mass makes us "missionary disciples"

We began these reflections on the Mass by quoting the words of the great Orthodox theologian Alexander Schmemann:

When I say I am going to church, it means I am going into the assembly of the faithful in order, together with them, to *constitute the Church*, in order to be what I became on the day of my baptism – a member, in the fullest, absolute meaning of the term, of the body of Christ.[26]

When we leave the church after Mass we don't forget our Christian identity. The Eucharist that we have just celebrated and shared conforms us more intimately to the Lord Jesus, making us all one body with him. And to us, his body, as we leave the Mass, Jesus says, "Go... make disciples of all the nations" (Matthew 28:19).

---

25 *Evangelii Nuntiandi*, 75.

26 Alexander Schmemann, *The Eucharist: Sacrament of the Kingdom* (New York: St Vladimir's Seminary Press, 2000), p. 23.

We bring the grace of our Eucharistic celebration and communion with Christ with us. We remember that Christ was there to welcome us as we entered the sacred assembly, our Sunday congregation, for the celebration of Mass. It was he who invited us to take our place at the table of the word of God where God our Father spoke to us and encouraged us. We stood together as one body and professed our faith as we said the Creed. Then, as our gifts of bread and wine were being presented to the priest at the altar, we reminded ourselves that these gifts represented us and "all that is within us", and we offered ourselves to God. During the great Eucharistic Prayer the priest imposed his hands over our gifts of bread and wine and prayed, "Make holy, therefore, these gifts, we pray, by sending down your Spirit upon them like the dewfall, so that they may become for us the Body and Blood of our Lord Jesus Christ."[27] In grateful amazement at the mystery of our faith, present on the altar through the power of the Holy Spirit and the words of Christ, we responded, "We proclaim your Death, O Lord, and profess your Resurrection until you come again." The priest invoked the Holy Spirit again and prayed, "Grant that we, who are nourished by the Body and Blood of your Son and filled with his Holy Spirit, may become one body, one spirit in Christ."[28] We renewed our faith in the amazing truth that, just as the bread and wine that represented us before God, through the power of the Holy Spirit, became for us the very Body and Blood of Christ, so now, through that same Holy Spirit, we become the body of Christ in this world. In the words of St Augustine we remembered:

> If you are the body and members of Christ, then it is your sacrament that is placed on the table of the Lord; it is your sacrament that you receive.[29]

We stood together, acknowledging that we are brothers and sisters as we said the Our Father, and then we shared the sign of peace

---

27 Eucharistic Prayer II.
28 Eucharistic Prayer III.
29 St Augustine, cited in *Catechism of the Catholic Church*, 1396.

that binds us together. After that we were all invited to the table of the Body of the Lord to receive Holy Communion, through which we become one with Christ and are filled with the Holy Spirit. It is from the table of the Lord that we are sent forth, not as isolated individuals but as the body of Christ, with the words, "Go and announce the Gospel of the Lord." If we are willing to announce the Gospel by the way we live as Christ's "missionary disciples", the Holy Spirit will give us the words or the actions that will make Christ known. We will be Christ's faithful, "missionary disciples" in our world. We will become the Eucharist we celebrate.